The Evil That Men Do

By the same author

One Was Not Enough
Motive to Murder

The Evil That Men Do

Twenty Man-made Murders

GEORGINA LLOYD

ROBERT HALE · LONDON

© Georgina Lloyd 1989
First published in Great Britain 1989

Robert Hale Limited
Clerkenwell House
Clerkenwell Green
London EC1R 0HT

British Library Cataloguing in Publication Data

Lloyd, Georgina
 The evil that men do
 1. Murder, 1820–1980
 I. Title
 364.1′523′09034

ISBN 0-7090-3530-6

Photoset in North Wales by
Derek Doyle & Associates, Mold, Clwyd.
Printed in Great Britain by
St Edmundsbury Press Ltd, Bury St Edmunds, Suffolk,
and bound by WBC Limited.

Contents

Introduction   7
1. A Mother-in-Law's Tongue   11
2. The Fireside Hearth Killer   27
3. The Doctor's Dilemma   37
4. A Slight Misunderstanding   47
5. The Toy Soldier   53
6. The Pillbox Murder   59
7. Hospital of Horror   67
8. Murder in the Blue Mountains   77
9. Two of a Kind   85
10. Beauty in Distress   91
11. The Melbourne Strangler   99
12. A Forensic Triumph   107
13. 'If at First you Don't Succeed …'   117
14. The Desert Killer   133
15. The Pressure Cooker Murder   137
16. The Man who Blew up Trains   145
17. The Coffin Case   149
18. A Family Conspiracy   153
19. Spelling was his Undoing   159
20. A Man called Smith   169

Author's Introduction

> 'The evil that men do lives after them'.
> William Shakespeare, *Julius Caesar*

The above quotation is as true today as it was in Shakespeare's day. In fact, there has never been a time, from antiquity until now, when it was not true.

The Bible is full of examples, as well as the holy books of other religions. History abounds with them, often on a massive scale. To cite only one example, the evil wrought by one man, Adolf Hitler, still rebounds on the families of his victims in our own generation.

There have been a few cases where the evil done by one man, or men, has resulted in far-reaching changes in the law. These may or may not have been for the better, but in most cases they have at least simplified legal procedures for the judges and counsel faced with the task of giving criminals a fair trial. The most famous of all these is probably the M'Naghten Rules of 1843.

In that year a Scot from Glasgow named Daniel M'Naghten shot Edward Drummond, the private secretary to Sir Robert Peel, the Prime Minister, in a London street, in the mistaken belief that his victim was Sir Robert, who he believed had been persecuting him. This was impossible, since Sir Robert had never even heard of Daniel M'Naghten. The assassin was suffering from persecution mania, the delusion now generally known as paranoia, in an acute form.

M'Naghten was tried for murder at the Old Bailey when medical evidence was put forward to show his state of mind. His defence was brilliantly conducted by Alexander Cockburn (later Lord Chief Justice of England), who argued that the accused had a background of insanity and at the time of the shooting he did not know that what he was doing was wrong. The jury acquitted him on these grounds. After the trial, the House of Lords, bowing to public concern, exercised their constitutional right to consult the judges on the law as it related to insanity in criminal cases. The judges' decisions became known as the M'Naghten Rules.

The main points of these Rules are that the jury must be told that every man is presumed sane until the contrary is proved to their satisfaction, and that to establish a defence on the grounds of insanity it must be shown that at the time of committing the offence the accused was, to use the terms of the Rules, 'labouring under such a defect of reason from disease of the mind as not to know the nature and quality of his act or, if he did know it, that he did not know that what he was doing was wrong.'

The Rules have been applied in several notable trials up to the present time, often with controversial results. Following the case of Ronald True, a murderer who was committed to Broadmoor in 1922, a committee was appointed to report on the laws regarding insanity, but the M'Naghten Rules have survived unchanged, and have also been adopted in most British Commonwealth countries and most of the United States. The true insanity of the accused must, however, be proved in a medical sense, and murderers who cunningly maintain that they were 'driven by voices' and use other ploys to simulate insanity, do not qualify to be deemed legally insane.

The criterion of knowing right from wrong still applies, but nowadays medical testimony is playing an increasingly vital role. The concept of 'diminished responsibility' is a direct result of this, the problem having always been to decide what degree of mental disorder has to be present in order to absolve a person from criminal responsibility.

Nearer to our own times has been the admission of evidence to prove 'system' in a trial provided that this has a direct bearing on the offence, or offences, with which a defendant has been charged. Briefly, if an offender is charged with, for example, murder by poisoning, and he or she is known to have poisoned, or attempted to poison, other persons previously, this may be put in evidence if it would tend to prove that the defendant is a 'systematic' poisoner – in other words, the use of poison is his preferred method of killing and he does not resort to the rope, the knife or the gun. A modern case of this kind was that of Graham Young, the St Albans poisoner.

The case of George Joseph Smith, with which I have concluded this book, is a classic example of 'system'. Once having drowned his bride in her bath and seen it as an easy way of attaining his ends which he was able to get away with, he employed the same method on two further occasions. If he had not been brought to book after the third drowning he would undoubtedly have used the same method again as opportunity occurred and the risk was worth while.

Apart from these legal repercussions, however, the evil that men do lives after them in the effects their crimes have on society. At the most immediate level, the family of a victim is bereaved or, in the case of a multiple murderer, the families of several victims. Others in their circle, too, are more indirectly affected: friends, teachers, pastors, employers, colleagues. Then there is the insidious influence of some kinds of criminals on other, often younger, persons who may have contact with them: the men who lure young girls and boys into prostitution and drug abuse are a case in point. The ripples spread outwards in ever-widening circles. The evil does not stop with the individuals who perpetrate it; everyone they touch is affected in some way. And therein lies the central truth of Shakespeare's famous line.

Georgina Lloyd

1 A Mother-in-Law's Tongue

Mrs Gregory, like many other respectable middle-class mothers before and since, naturally wanted her daughter Beatrice to make a good match. A widow herself, Mrs Gregory had been left in less than comfortable circumstances, and to make ends meet she had to take in dressmaking. Beatrice, who was barely nineteen, worked in a factory in London where they lived in their modest rented home. Mrs Gregory was hoping that her daughter, who was well-mannered, quiet and not bad-looking, would somehow contrive to meet a suitor who could offer her something better than what she had now – not, perhaps, a rich man, or one of the lords she was so fond of reading about in the romantic novelettes of the day, but someone of what was called in those days 'good breeding' who had a good steady job and a bank account and did not live from hand to mouth.

Mrs Gregory felt that their drab North London suburb was not the most likely place for Beatrice to meet such a contender for her hand, and since the annual fortnight's holiday was looming she gave the matter a little more thought than usual and decided to choose a place where they would be more likely to meet people of the kind to whom her daughter could be introduced and who could, perhaps, in their turn introduce Beatrice to someone suitable. For some unaccountable reason Hastings in Sussex was the choice of venue for the holiday, although there were probably more likely places. But it was in Hastings that Mrs Gregory was able to locate a modest hotel at a cost she could afford from her carefully saved earnings. Admittedly the view of the sea was possible only if one climbed up on to the roof, but ...

So the pair took the train to the place where Harold had faced William in battle and been worsted. The summer that year was very hot and Beatrice found this very trying, preferring to spend much time in their room on the fifth floor. She suffered from recurrent headaches, and looked pale and drawn.

'You are not getting enough fresh air,' her mother advised. 'What is the point of a seaside holiday if you just sit and mope indoors? You should get out more. The beach is a good place for a walk.'

'I am fed up with the beach,' the girl replied.

'Then why not go and watch the fishing boats in the harbour,' was the rejoinder. 'It would make a nice change. You could take your box Brownie and then you'd have some nice snaps to show the girls at the factory when you get home.'

'I've been to the harbour,' Beatrice replied. 'The place stinks of fish.'

'Oh, dear,' her mother reproved, 'that doesn't sound very ladylike!'

'Mother,' the girl snapped, 'I have a headache and I don't feel very ladylike. Anyway, I was just telling you the truth about what I think. What would you have me say – that the harbour smells of roses?'

Mrs Gregory gave a forced smile while her knitting-needles clicked in disapproval. 'Roses! You ought to go and walk in the park. There are flower gardens there you would really enjoy. Go and see them tomorrow. You haven't been there yet, have you?'

'No, Mother. All right – I'll go to the park tomorrow.'

Beatrice Gregory loved flowers, and in Hastings' Alexandra Park she had her fill of them. The roses, ornamental shrubs, annual and perennial beds and the neat lawns were the pride and joy of the gardeners whose job it was to keep them beautiful. Beatrice was completely absorbed in her enjoyment of them.

Rapt in her attention, Beatrice did not notice the shadow that fell across the path nor was she aware of the presence of another person beside her, until a voice spoke. 'Aren't they beautiful? The gardens here are the envy of other

A Mother-in-Law's Tongue

seaside resorts. Only the other day I told the head gardener what a good job he was doing.'

Beatrice turned and saw a good-looking, well-dressed young fellow. He was well-spoken, and seemed respectable enough. What was the harm in chatting to the young stranger? After all, this was a seaside holiday, and holiday acquaintanceships, then as now, tended to be pursued with a good deal less formality than at other times. After her holiday had ended she would never see him again.

She chatted easily with the affable stranger, strolling along the neat paths beside the manicured lawns and well-tended flower-beds where not one weed dared raise its head. Soon it was time to return to the hotel for tea, and she took leave of her companion. He had not asked to see her again, nor had his behaviour been in the least forward – in short, he seemed to be a perfect gentleman.

The next morning Beatrice was in good spirits and it was obvious that the outing to Alexandra Park had done her some good. But it was now her mother who was complaining of a headache. She asked her daughter for some aspirin. Beatrice, however, had run out of supplies of the drug, so Mrs Gregory asked her to nip out after breakfast when the shops would be open to get some.

Beatrice came to a chemist's shop about half-way along the row of shops which formed a crescent a few dozen yards from the hotel. As she went up to the counter, the face which appeared on the other side was familiar. It was her erstwhile acquaintance of the park.

'Why, hello! Fancy seeing you again!' he said, tugging at a stiff white collar he was wearing. 'Did you know I worked here?'

'No, of course not,' replied Beatrice, blushing furiously. 'My mother just sent me out for some aspirin for her headache. I certainly did not know you worked here – I thought you were in Hastings on holiday, like me.'

'What a coincidence!' the young man said as he put a small bottle of aspirin tablets into a brown paper bag and gave Beatrice change from the shilling she had tendered. 'I hope now that we are better acquainted, we shall be able to see each other again. My name's Arthur – Arthur Devereux. What's yours?'

'Beatrice Gregory,' the girl answered, a slow flush rising to her cheeks as she realized that this good-looking chemist's assistant was taking more than just a passing interest in her.

'Perhaps we could meet at six o'clock after I have finished work,' he suggested. 'We could go for a walk and a cup of tea afterwards.'

'Thank you, I should like that,' Beatrice agreed. This personable young fellow was not, perhaps, one of the dashing heroes of Rider Haggard or Mrs Wood, but at least he was real. She wouldn't have to take him back to the library later.

Mrs Gregory was non-committal. The young man was taken to meet her, and the three of them had tea together in one of the olde-worlde tearooms when Arthur could afford to take them. Gradually Mrs Gregory began to appreciate his good points: he was punctual, courteous, behaved like a gentleman, and had a steady job with prospects. She was realistic enough to know that in their humble position in life there was no possibility of meeting one of the titled fraternity, or a landed member of the hunting set. And when Arthur, shortly before their holiday was about to come to an end, eventually summoned up the courage to declare his intentions, Mrs Gregory decided that perhaps it would be best not to set her sights too high but to settle for what she could get. After all, the young man seemed respectable enough. And it was obvious that he and her daughter had fallen headlong in love with each other. Her daughter's happiness was, as always, her major consideration, coupled with the suitability of a prospective husband.

Just before the end of the holiday the young couple announced their engagement (Arthur had secretly borrowed money from his uncle to enable him to purchase the ring). Mrs Gregory naturally expected that the engagement would last a year, or even two, according to the usual custom in those times. Such a period gave the prospective husband time to save for a home, and the bride-to-be time to prepare her trousseau. There would be linen to be hand-embroidered, wrapped in tissue-paper and laid lovingly in her bottom drawer. Mrs Gregory was, therefore, understandably dismayed when Arthur told her that he wished to marry Beatrice as soon as possible.

'But you are both so young!' Mrs Gregory pointed out. 'Beatrice is not yet twenty, and you are only eighteen. Don't you think you should wait at least until you are both over twenty-one before you marry? That would at least give you time to save for a home.' Then, almost as an afterthought, she added, 'You have known each other only a fortnight!'

'Ah, yes, Mrs Gregory, I do see your point,' the plausible Arthur replied. 'But we are so in love. We want to be together all the time. And we can only do that if we're married.'

'That's true,' Mrs Gregory said.

'If I stayed here in Hastings, and you and Beatrice went back to London as, of course, you will do after your holiday,' Arthur continued relentlessly, 'I would never see her. If I were saving for a home, as you say, I'd never be able to afford to come up to London regularly to see her. And you'd not come here again until your next seaside holiday – another year, no doubt. Who knows? Beatrice might even meet someone else!'

'It certainly would be difficult,' conceded Mrs Gregory.

'What I have in mind,' the glib Arthur said, 'is to come up to London and look for another job. In London, of course, my wages would be higher than they are here. And my boss would give me a good reference. Then I'd look for a furnished place to rent to start with. We'd marry in London, and then we'd start looking for a proper home. And I could save more, of course, than I could if I stayed here.'

With this ploy Arthur Devereux finally persuaded the half-reluctant Mrs Gregory to give her consent to the marriage. Arthur's parents were both dead, and his aunt and uncle, with whom he lived, needed little persuasion to give their consent to his under-age wedding. They would be glad to get him off their hands. They had several children of their own, all younger than Arthur. It would be one less mouth to feed. Arthur did not contribute very much to their household expenses – he spent far too much, they said, on clothes and gallivanting about.

Beatrice Gregory and Arthur Devereux were duly married, and went to live in a small rented terraced house in one of the drabber back streets of Kilburn. Arthur's new job – again as a chemist's shop-assistant – was of course better paid than the job he had held in the South Coast resort town – but not much. They did without a honeymoon – they could not afford it – and Beatrice went back to her factory job. She knew that if and when a family came along in due course, anything she could save from her meagre wages would be useful. Three could not live as cheaply as two – at least not the first time, when one had to provide a pram, a cot, and baby clothes. It was of course easier when one had another child, as these things could be passed on. The pram and cot would be second-hand, and she would be able to save on the clothes by buying material and wool and making them herself. Knitting and sewing were things she was good at. Working as she did in a shirt factory, there was often a bargain to be had in spare pieces of material and imperfect shirts. The latter came in useful for Arthur at a fraction of shop prices. And spare pieces left over from making workmen's flannel shirts would be just the right size to make up into warm baby garments.

It was not long before Beatrice found herself pregnant. She stayed at her job for as long as she could, and in due time gave birth to a boy, who was named Stanley. Arthur was overjoyed at having a son, and made up his mind that the new addition to the family should have all the best of everything as far as was humanly possible. Unfortunately all these grandiose plans cost money, and Arthur Devereux soon found himself deeply in debt, a state of affairs caused entirely by his extravagance. He had developed a neurotic obsession about Stanley and the role the child was playing in his life. He became not merely a doting father, but literally besotted. Even the baby's own mother remonstrated with him that he was making himself ridiculous. Already he was the laughing-stock of all his friends. He even tried to take the baby into the pub to show him off, until barred by the landlord.

Beatrice, in desperation, unable to return to her job, sewed and knitted. She took refuge at her mother's who, fortunately, did not live too far away; even so, she usually walked instead of taking the bus to save the fare. Often she could not take the baby to her mother's because Arthur wanted to keep Stanley with him. He could hardly bear to let the child out of his sight. Mrs Gregory thought her son-in-law a very odd fellow indeed. Almost the only way she could see her grandson was to go to the young couple's home herself. And she, who had so much wanted her daughter to better herself, was appalled every time she saw the drab, tiny house in the street which was little more than a slum. It did not even have a backyard, never mind a garden where the child would be able to play later on without danger from the traffic.

If Beatrice was in a good mood and wanted to please her husband, all she had to do was wheel Stanley in his pram to the chemist's shop where Arthur worked, and the underpaid and overworked assistant's face would light up. But one day, on one of these visits, Beatrice brought him some news at which the light definitely went out of his features. She told him that she was going to have another baby.

'My God! What are we going to do?' he exploded. 'We cannot afford any more children just now. It will be a couple of years before they make me manager here.' But Arthur's real fear was that the new arrival would make less money available to be lavished upon Stanley. Instead of giving him cause for rejoicing, the news of his impending second fatherhood cast him into a deep gloom.

Beatrice had no inkling that she would give birth to twins. Medical examinations in those days were not as thorough as they are now. And when the two boys arrived, the shock to Arthur Devereux was even more than it was to his wife.

The twins were given names straight out of the knightly tales from Arthur's namesake of the Round Table: Lawrence Roland and Evelyn Lancelot. The names, with their echoes of far-off chivalry, sounded faintly incongruous in the shabby house where lines of faded off-white napkins hung disconsolately from the lines stretched across the kitchen and the two babies vied with one another in screaming during the night until their exhausted mother pacified them with the breast.

Arthur Devereux became a moody man as he cast about for ways and means to alleviate the financial situation, which in his eyes centred on the fact that money spent for the benefit of the twins was, in effect, being diverted from Stanley. He asked his boss for a rise, and was refused. He asked his uncle for a loan, and was reminded that he had not yet repaid the previous one for the purchase of the engagement-ring. He asked his bank for an overdraft, and was informed that overdrafts were not given to customers who had less than two pounds in their account.

Arthur's obsession, and the blow Fate had dealt him in the shape of two bawling infants so soon after the arrival of Stanley, seemed to unhinge him completely. He began to accuse his wife of – as he put it – being in league with the twins against him and Stanley. In vain did she tell him that he was being absurd. She was doing her best in difficult circumstances, she pointed out. She was a faithful wife and a good mother. What more could he ask? In league with his own children against him? – what rubbish!

Arthur's mental disturbance affected his performance at work and he was fired from his job. For weeks he brooded as he drew only the few shillings' dole. Then he found another job, at yet another chemist's, and for a time things improved slightly. But this new job, too, did not last very long, and Arthur's resources again hit a new low. Beatrice spent more and more time at her mother's with the twins, while Arthur spent his time with Stanley. And while Beatrice asked her mother for advice on how to save her marriage from becoming a complete shambles, Arthur indulged in impossible daydreams, such as sending Stanley to a private school, and later to college and to university. At least, he would have more of a chance if he could somehow unload his other responsibilities. But how? Divorce? He could not afford it – and anyway he had no grounds whatsoever. What about doing a midnight flit and emigrating with Stanley to America? The formalities would take too long, official documents would arrive and Beatrice would become suspicious. Besides, he could not afford it. No, he must think of a better plan …

One day Arthur, who had fortuitously found another new job in a chemist's, came home with some good news.

A Mother-in-Law's Tongue

'I've found a cheaper place to live,' he told his wife. 'It's not far from here, and the rent's only half what we pay here.'

'What's the snag?' Beatrice said.

'Ah, yes. There's another family living in the house. But they seem all right. Nice couple, two kids at school. Irish, I think. Anyway, they've got the upstairs flat on the second floor. We'd have the bottom part – two floors. And there's a backyard. Just a little one of course but you know what they say – half a loaf is better than no bread.'

'Sounds too good to be true,' Beatrice said. She had lost most of her illusions by this time and was no longer the romantic young girl who viewed life through rose-tinted spectacles. Although still only in her early twenties, she looked thirty-five.

The next day Arthur came home with a big black trunk. 'It's for moving,' he explained.

'We haven't much stuff to move,' Beatrice observed. 'You could have got a much smaller one than that.'

'Oh, I don't know,' he continued. 'It all adds up, you know, and when you start packing you often find a small one isn't big enough.'

Beatrice busied herself with ironing the babies' clothes. 'What about a cup of cocoa?' Arthur suggested. 'I'll make it – you needn't stop what you're doing.'

'Why cocoa? Have we run out of tea? I don't think so.'

'Yes, we have. I took the last packet to work. You know we have to provide our own.'

'You might've told me,' Beatrice protested. 'Then I could have borrowed some from my mother's.' She made a gesture of annoyance. 'Oh, all right, then – we'll have cocoa.'

'Give me the babies' bottles and I'll make some for them, too,' Arthur said.

'Don't make it too strong for them,' the harassed mother said. 'Just a little – the rest milk.'

Out in the kitchen, Arthur Devereux poured a lethal mixture of cocoa and morphine which he had stolen from the shop. He gave a cup to his wife, and himself fed the two babies – an unprecedented thing for him to do. Stanley was asleep in bed upstairs. 'No point in waking him up to give him cocoa,' Arthur said.

The babies were the first to die, peacefully in their sleep. Then Beatrice said she felt very drowsy and would go and lie down. Arthur took the iron off its stand, and packed up the ironing-board. When he went upstairs, his wife was dead. It was a good job he was a knowledgeable chemist and dispenser, he thought to himself. No messy knives or choppers. No noisy gun. No unpleasant strangling or hanging jobs.

The bodies of his wife and two children were still warm as Arthur Devereux fetched the big trunk downstairs and bundled them into it. He locked the trunk and threw the key into the kitchen boiler. Then he went upstairs to bed, feeling very pleased with himself at his ingenuity in solving his most pressing problem. He looked in on the peacefully-sleeping Stanley. Now the boy's future was assured; he would be able to have a fine education, good clothes, everything he wanted. There would be no competitors for his rightful place in the world.

The next day Arthur whistled to himself as he cooked breakfast for himself and Stanley. When the milkman called, he paid the bill for the week and told him not to leave any more milk. 'My wife and the babies have gone on holiday,' he said. 'As for Stanley and myself, we can manage.'

After breakfast, Arthur washed up, then left the boy in another room with his toys while he attended to the trunk. First of all, he tied a stout rope he had procured firmly around it and knotted it; then he sealed all the edges with glue which he had bought for the purpose. Next he took Stanley to the house of a friend, with whom he left him while he undertook an urgent journey. He did not tell his friend what this journey was. But he told him that he would not be very long.

Arthur visited a large furniture removal and repository firm in Kensal Rise, which had warehouses there and in Harrow. He asked the foreman if he could call at his Kilburn home to pick up a large trunk full of books which he wanted put into storage while he was away from home for some time. He could not at present give them a date for his return. 'When is the earliest you can call and collect it?' he asked.

A Mother-in-Law's Tongue

'How about this afternoon? Will that do?'

'That will suit me very nicely,' Arthur replied. 'I shall be at home any time after two. I left my little boy with a neighbour while I popped out, so I will have to collect him and then cook our lunch, as my wife is at her mother's.' The foreman handed him a receipt for his first monthly payment, and Arthur promised to send the money when due for as many months as he would be away.

That afternoon, two hefty removal men carried the black trunk with its dreadful burden to their van from Arthur Devereux's house. 'Blimey!' said one. 'Wot you got in 'ere? Lead?'

'Books,' said Arthur Devereux without batting an eyelid.

'Must be the whole bloody public library!' the man replied.

As soon as the van had left, Arthur went out to see a second-hand dealer he knew and arranged with him to call and collect, also that same day, the pitiful furnishings which Beatrice had spent the last years of her young life polishing with such loving care. For these Arthur received a few pounds which would enable him to move and start a new life with Stanley. He would relocate to a different part of London, perhaps south of the Thames – a better neighbourhood, too. Kilburn was no place for Stanley.

Suiting action to the intentions, he called in another friendly neighbour to look after Stanley while he went out that same evening, took a bus and searched for rooms in the southern suburbs. He was successful, since rooms were then easy to find – in fact landladies were falling over themselves to find decent tenants. The average wage of a breadwinner in those days could be measured in shillings rather than pounds per week, and a lodger was the usual answer to help make ends meet. The neighbour who was baby-sitting Stanley was somewhat surprised to find the house empty save for a couple of rickety chairs, but the glib Arthur informed her that he was moving that same evening – which he did.

Arthur felt a new man in his new lodgings, which were clean and spacious. He had a new job lined up to start the following Monday, prior to which he had the rest of the week-end to buy a few sticks of essential second-hand furniture to supplement the sparse few items that enabled his new landlady to call her upper flat 'furnished'. There was actually a bathroom, shared with the owners of the house – no more trips to the public baths. And the landlady fell in love with the curly-headed Stanley, who had Beatrice's delicate fair colouring, at first sight. She would baby-sit him while Arthur was at work dishing out pills, potions, prescriptions and – possibly – poisons. But soon it would be time for Stanley to start school. Arthur already had in mind a smart private school not far away. The Head had agreed to reserve a place for Stanley. And at this interview Arthur had learned that one of the pupils was the grandson of a real live earl. Stanley would not need to hobnob with slum kids in Kilburn's back streets.

One day a letter arrived from Mrs Gregory. How on earth she had managed to ferret out his new address Arthur had no idea. She was a determined woman when she wanted to be. She complained that she had not seen her daughter for a few weeks and wondered if she was ill. Arthur wrote back to his mother-in-law, enjoying the sensation of power he felt as he told her that Beatrice was, indeed, not in the best of health – a masterpiece of understatement – and had gone to the country for a week or two with the twins to recuperate. He added that the upheaval of moving had been all too much for her.

Mrs Gregory was not a woman to be fobbed off. She replied by return demanding her daughter's address in the country. Arthur did not bother to reply. This produced the result that Mrs Gregory turned up on his doorstep in person, demanding the address, whereupon Arthur told her that his wife did not wish to be disturbed and that letter-writing upset her and was forbidden by her doctor. 'She will come home when she is better,' he added lamely, 'but I do not at present know when this will be.'

Mrs Gregory was not nearly so gullible as Arthur imagined. She could feel that there was something here that needed to be looked into. And look into it she did. First of all, she went to the family's old address in Kilburn, but the new tenants there had moved in only after her son-in-law had gone and had no idea where or even who they were. She struck more lucky, however, with a neighbour when she went systematically along the street making inquiries door-to-door. A woman remembered seeing a large furniture removal van bearing the name of the firm and its address in Kensal Rise outside the house on the day the family left. The woman, a Mrs Cassidy from County Cork, said she saw a large black trunk being carried to the van by two men.

Mrs Gregory was filled with a sense of foreboding. She felt that her daughter's protracted absence was more than just that – more a disappearance. She considered that the best place to start would be with the furniture removal and repository firm. When her son-in-law had shown her over his new abode, ostensibly to reassure her that Stanley now had much more comfortable surroundings, she had not noticed a black trunk anywhere in the house.

The foreman confirmed that they were holding a large black trunk for her son-in-law, who had given his correct name and address, and when sending the second monthly payment which was due a few days before her visit, he had given his correct new address and been sent a receipt. So far so good, but Mrs Gregory wished to know what the contents of the trunk were. The foreman told her that he was not allowed to open it to a third party without the authorization of a magistrate's warrant.

Mrs Gregory left the office and the foreman thought he had seen the last of a busybody, but he was soon proved wrong. The determined mother-in-law returned with a policeman bearing the necessary warrant to open the trunk.

The foreman stared aghast at the decomposing bodies: a woman and two small babies, jammed tightly into the trunk, fully-clothed. Mrs Gregory collapsed in hysterics. Even the policeman was visibly shaken. Scotland Yard were called in immediately, and Inspector Pollard was despatched to the Kensal Rise repository with two sergeants and another constable. The following morning the crime was in all the headlines. Arthur Devereux, jarred out of his complacency, was jolted into action. Grabbing Stanley, he took a train to the first place he could think of far enough from London – Coventry.

Arthur Devereux knew no other way of earning a living than being a chemist's assistant. Inspector Pollard knew that, as soon as the fugitive ran short of funds, that is the first thing he would do – get a new job. This would, again, be in a chemist's – Arthur was far too snobbish to take any old labouring job, even if it were more highly paid. And, before long, Pollard knew, he would be looking for a private school to put Stanley's name down for the following year when he would be five. In the meantime, he would have to find a woman able to look after the boy in the daytime while he was at work. All this, and more, he put together from information supplied by the indefatigable mother-in-law.

It took Pollard some little time before Arthur Devereux was traced to Coventry. He had no connections there, and the breakthrough came only after an observant booking-office clerk at Euston remembered the man without luggage, accompanied by a fair-haired boy, purchasing a ticket, one-way, to Coventry on the day the crime made the headlines. This booking-clerk had a phenomenal memory for faces and Pollard wished he worked in Scotland Yard, where he would be much more useful. After all, anybody could sell railway tickets ...

Once pinpointed in Coventry, it was a simple matter to ferret out the fugitive, who now called himself Sidney Andrews and referred to Stanley by his middle name of George. All Pollard had to do was to make the rounds of all the chemists' shops in the city and, when he struck oil with the description of the wanted man, to obtain his address from the manager.

Confronted with the Yard man, the affable Arthur feigned complete astonishment. He invited the policeman in for a cup of tea. 'Not me, chum,' he said. 'You must have made a mistake and got me muddled with someone else. I don't know anything about any trunk. I've never lived in Kilburn. I don't know what you're talking about.'

Pollard was not to be put off. Like Mrs Gregory, he did not give up easily. He brought Arthur back to London, after arranging for the woman who was looking after Stanley to continue to do so until they could find a place for him in a children's home. This made Arthur very angry. The separation was more than he had bargained for.

He was left for his anger to subside sufficiently to allow a further interview, during which Pollard gave him some advice which evidently had some effect on him, for after this he agreed to make a voluntary statement. In this he said that his wife had killed the twins and committed suicide, having already threatened to do so several times on account of the hunger and poverty besetting her when Arthur had been several weeks out of a job. He had come home one evening after looking for work, he said, to find them all dead in bed. When asked how they had died, he said they must have drunk weedkiller or disinfectant.

'Isn't it true that they died from morphine poisoning?' the Yard man persisted.

'Morphine? I don't keep morphine in the house. Why should I? I dispense it to doctors at the shop – that is, when I have a job – but I was unemployed at the time. Where would she have got morphine?'

'We think you know more than you have told us about the manner of their death,' Pollard said.

'Imagine my position, sir,' Arthur said. 'My wife had poisoned the twins and herself. I am a chemist's assistant and dispenser. I had been previously in a position to obtain poison. No one would be prepared to believe me that I was not a murderer ... I lost my head. I decided that the best thing to do would be to hush up the whole thing. So I bought the trunk and placed the bodies in it, and left it in store. That's the truth. If you don't believe me I can't help it. I am innocent. I loved my wife and children. Why should I kill them? Admittedly, times were hard. But then they are harder still for lots of people who have far more children than we do – than we *did*. And they don't go round killing their wives and children.'

Pollard was able to prove not only motive but malice aforethought – in other words, premeditated murder – because several witnesses were found who had seen the trunk being delivered to the house *before* Beatrice and the twins were seen alive for the last time by various neighbours. Arthur Devereux was committed for trial at the Old Bailey. He was defended by Mr Charles Elliott, and the prosecutor was Sir Charles Matthews, later to become a famous Director of Public Prosecutions.

The trial judge, Mr Justice Ridley, was not the kind of judge to be stampeded. He told the defence that no weight should be attached to the screaming headlines in the Press, and that he was sure in his own mind that the jury would prove themselves to be supremely impartial in their consideration of the evidence, in the true traditions of British criminal justice.

In the last resort, Arthur Devereux put forward a defence of insanity, citing his desperation at being unemployed, his inability to support his family and his anguish at watching his family go hungry. He admitted having smuggled morphine into his home from his previous employers' stocks, but claimed it was only to drug his wife and children when they could not sleep through hunger. He had, he said, obviously miscalculated the dose.

A psychiatrist called to examine the defendant to establish whether he was legally sane was not fooled by the prisoner's bluff. He quickly pronounced him sane in law. There was a great deal of evidence to back him up; for instance, premeditated murder could be proved by a letter Arthur Devereux had written while his wife was still alive to a firm of chemists in Hull advertising for a senior assistant. In this letter he had described himself as a widower. He was also proved to have bought the trunk at a time when he was still in employment, thus giving the 'hardship mercy killing' theory a rather hard knock on the head.

The jury did not take very long to find him guilty – they were out less than an hour – and Mr Justice Ridley sentenced him to death. He was hanged at Pentonville on 15 August 1905.

2 The Fireside Hearth Killer

1892 was not exactly a boom year in Melbourne, Australia. The slowly-developing suburb of Windsor, like the rest of the city, was affected severely by mass unemployment, breadlines, soup-kitchens and hunger marches. Few people wanted to move into the area and, with few jobs available, a good many people moved out. As a result, there were large numbers of empty houses; nobody would buy them, and rents were low because the only people likely to rent them were the self-employed or the elderly who were not dependent on an outside job for their sustenance.

John Stafford was the owner of one such house, situated at 57 Andrew Street, Windsor. With an estimated 9,000 unoccupied houses in Melbourne, he considered himself very lucky indeed when a prospective tenant turned up on his doorstep. He agreed to accompany her to the house, with the key, immediately, and together they trudged along the almost deserted streets to view the property. The house had been vacant for three weeks. It was now Thursday, 3 March.

John Stafford stood in the hall with the keys in his hand. 'Have a good look round while we're here,' he said. 'I'm not going to be free again for another day or two.' The woman traversed the length of the hall, popping her head into all the rooms which opened off on either side. 'Peculiar smell this place has,' she observed.

'Well, the place has been shut up for three weeks,' Stafford replied. 'A bit musty.' He coughed uneasily. 'If you open all the windows and scrub the place out it'll be O.K.'

'Oh, it's not that,' the woman said. 'It's something

worse than that. Seems to be coming from that room there.' And she pointed to one of the smaller rooms, from which she had made a somewhat precipitate retreat. Stafford could see his hopes of securing a new tenancy fading by the minute.

She had hardly left the premises when the owner decided to investigate further. After all, he could hardly expect to obtain another tenant if the place stank. Must be the drains. Blocked, no doubt. He'd have to fetch a plumber. More expense ...

Entering the offending room, Stafford had to admit that his erstwhile prospective tenant had been absolutely right. No one in his or her right senses would rent a house which could produce a smell as foul as that. At the same time, he noticed that the fireside hearthstones were raised a couple of inches or so above the surrounding level of the floor. This was not right – surely the hearthstones should be flush with the floor? He decided to call on his letting agent, a Mr Bernard Moxon of Commercial Road, Prahran. Asking for details of the last tenant, he was informed that it had been a Mr Albert Williams, who with his wife Emily had moved in after paying a month's rent in advance. Only a few days after they had moved in they had disappeared, and no one knew where they had gone. Very odd, Stafford thought. Very odd indeed ...

After some discussion, Stafford and Moxon decided to inform the police and ask them to investigate. March is high summer in Australia, and the odour was hourly becoming worse owing to the heat and also to the fact that the house had been closed for so long without ventilation. And since the front door of the premises had been opened the smell had penetrated to the neighbouring dwellings and brought out the tenants with queries as to the state of the drains. Something must be done, and soon, they said. They did not want their children catching typhoid.

From the neighbours, the police learned that Mr and Mrs Williams were a couple not long arrived from England, and that he was a toolmaker by trade. He was of medium height, probably in his middle to late thirties, fair-haired and bearded. Mrs Williams was small and of a shy and retiring disposition, never saying very much. One neighbour volunteered the information that a few weeks previously, shortly before the couple had moved, an ironmonger had made a delivery at the house of a spade and trowel, and a builders' merchant had delivered a sack of cement and a sack of sand.

Bernard Moxon, the estate agent, assured the police that the drains were unlikely to be blocked, because they had been inspected just before the couple had moved in, along with the drains to all the properties in the street, during the course of inspections by the newly formed sanitary commission. They were determined to keep typhoid out of Melbourne.

Two sergeants, William Considine and Henry Cawsey, were put in charge of the investigation in the house and borrowed the keys. It was decided to dig up the uneven hearthstones and try to locate the cause of the stench. The cement underlying the surface stones was not very thick, and a few blows with a pickaxe at the edges cracked it wide open. Beneath the jagged pieces lay the body of a young woman in a nightdress. She might once have been pretty, but not now ...

A post-mortem showed that the woman, aged about thirty, had been killed with a heavy blow to the head with a blunt instrument, which had smashed her skull. In addition, her throat had been cut for good measure. The pathologist stated that, in his opinion, the body had been buried between three and four weeks. There were no signs of blood in any other part of the house.

In the fireplace, police found a luggage ticket which had been torn in half. This testified that Williams had arrived in Melbourne from the United Kingdom on 9 December 1891 on board the *Kaiser Wilhelm II*. His name appeared on the ship's passenger list as Albert Williams, and he was accompanied by his wife, Emily. Ships' officers remembered him owing to his distinguished-looking appearance and his stories of exploits in various parts of the world. But it was to a pauper's grave that his wife's body was committed, a large crowd gathering in Melbourne's central cemetery, while her husband was being sought by the law. A warrant had been issued for his arrest, and accounts of the 'Windsor Tragedy' were making headlines throughout the state.

Meantime, more detachments of police were sent to the house to examine its contents for clues. The missing husband, when he fled, had not bothered to sell his furniture or otherwise deal with his possessions. The police found a large family Bible, and the inscription on the flyleaf informed them that it had once been the property of a Mrs Mather, of Rainhill, Lancashire, in England. They found no clues to the present whereabouts of the fugitive, so they made inquiries at the docks, in case their quarry had booked a passage to England. No such passage had been booked, but an astute shipping clerk remembered a man answering to Williams's description booking a passage from Melbourne to Fremantle on 23 January. He had, however, given his name as 'Baron Swanston'. The investigating officers exchanged knowing nods. The retailer of the tales of high adventure – most of which could be taken with a large handful of salt – with a drink in one hand and a fat cigar in the other on the deck of the *Kaiser Wilhelm II* – had now acquired a title, no doubt self-appointed. It figured, as they say.

The shipping clerk, it seemed, had particularly remembered the 'Baron' on account of a casual conversation they had had at the time of the booking, when his customer mentioned that he was taking up an appointment as a mining engineer in Western Australia. This nattily attired Englishman with the fashionable side-whiskers looked about as much like a rugged mining engineer, he thought, as a platypus looks like a kangaroo.

When the shipping clerk saw the newspapers, he immediately realised that the 'Baron' was none other than Williams, currently the most wanted man in Australia. He contacted the police, and not long afterwards Williams, still protesting that he was Baron Swanston and professing no knowledge of any crime, was arrested at the mining settlement of Southern Cross, 240 miles From Perth.

News of Williams's arrest came as a great shock to a nineteen-year-old girl named Kate Roundsfell, who had just arrived in Melbourne from New South Wales on her way to Western Australia. She told detectives that she had met 'Baron Swanston' on board ship travelling from

The Fireside Hearth Killer

Adelaide to Sydney while she was on her way to stay with her sister in Bathurst. The 'Baron' had joined the ship on 12 January and lost no time in paying her courtly and well-mannered attentions. When the ship docked at Sydney, Kate Roundsfell discovered that no more trains to Bathurst were running that day. She booked into the Wentworth Hotel, and Williams booked a room in the same establishment.

The following afternoon they spent on a sightseeing tour of Sydney, and that same evening the 'Baron' asked her to marry him, to her astonishment: 'I've known you only two days,' she pointed out with some diffidence though not unmindful that if she did marry this charming stranger she would become a baroness, no less. Lady Swanston – that wouldn't sound too bad.

The next morning they took the train to Bathurst where Kate introduced her new suitor to her sister. The sister was suitably impressed by the worldly, suave 'Baron Swanston', who took Kate for a buggy ride, proposed to her again, and was formally accepted. He then made arrangements to leave, in order, he said, to take up his new appointment at the mines, and as soon as he was settled in he would send for her.

On 10 March, Kate received a telegram which read 'Come at once' from her fiancé. She left Bathurst on the afternoon train for Melbourne, from where she could join a ship to Western Australia. For her stay in Melbourne a friend of the family had booked her a room in a hotel.

Shortly before the time Kate would have reached Melbourne according to the railway timetable, her sister in Bathurst received a visit from the police, who showed her a photograph of Albert Williams, wanted for murder. She recognised him at once and immediately sent off a telegram to her sister, which Kate found awaiting her in her hotel in Melbourne. It read simply, 'For God's sake go no further'.

Kate was, naturally, mystified completely, and wired her sister for details. On her way back to the hotel from the post office she purchased a newspaper. The headline screamed at her in black banner letters: 'WINDSOR MURDERER ARRESTED IN WESTERN AUSTRALIA ...

Albert Williams, alias Baron Swanston, has been arrested at Southern Cross, W.A., for the murder of his wife at Windsor, Melbourne ...' Kate collapsed in the street on reading the news. She was helped to her hotel by passers-by, and a doctor was called.

In the meantime, the police had been busy. Knowing that Williams was English, and having proof of the date of his arrival in Australia, they were intrigued at the reference to a Mrs Mather, of Rainhill, Lancashire, on the flyleaf of the family Bible he had left behind. Who was Mrs Mather? Could she be his mother-in-law? To add fuel to the flame, a constable searching the dustbin behind the house at 57 Andrew Street found a screwed-up invitation card to a dinner given by Albert Williams at the Commercial Hotel, Rainhill, in August 1891. Police intuition motivated them to enlist the support of the English police to investigate the background of Albert Williams and to ascertain the relevance of the mysterious Mrs Mather. It might throw some light on this man they now had in their custody.

Mrs Mather as the police surmised, proved to be the mother of Emily Williams, the murdered woman. She and her daughter had met Williams when he called about a house Mrs Mather had to let. He told her that he wanted to rent it on behalf of his employer, a Colonel Brooks, who would be arriving shortly from service in India. Williams leased the house, Dinham Villa, and lived there himself; the mythical Colonel Brooks never did turn up.

Williams spent freely, told thrilling tales of his adventures abroad to those who would listen in the local pubs, and assiduously courted Mrs Mather's daughter, who was much younger than Williams. Mrs Mather had her misgivings, and considered that Williams was too old for Emily, but there was little she could do, and the couple married on 22 September 1891. They proposed to emigrate to Australia, and shortly before leaving Williams threw a lavish party at the house in Rainhill.

Some curious and disturbing facts came to light as the police were nosing about Rainhill, making enquiries of various neighbours in Lawton Street, where Dinham Villa was situated. Williams was well known in the area:

Rainhill is quite a small place even today, and it was considerably smaller in 1892, situated about four miles from St Helen's. On the eve of his departure he was known to have defrauded several tradesmen by ordering goods on credit, obviously with no intention of paying for them. Then, earlier, he had mentioned his sister, a widow with four children, who would be coming to stay with him for a week for a holiday from their home in London. The woman duly arrived, the children ranging in age from seven to eleven. After their week's holiday, they apparently left suddenly and were never seen again, and no one had seen or heard them leave.

Finally, Mrs Mather herself came up with something that clinched the evidence for the police. She remembered that on signing the lease for Dinham Villa Williams had asked her permission to relay the floor in the big kitchen-cum-living-room 'before Colonel Brooks arrived'. He had gone on to point out that 'Colonel Brooks would not be prepared to live in a house where the rooms had uneven floors'. She thought this a most curious remark at the time, since as far as she was aware the floors in all the rooms were as level as they could and should be. What she did not realize was that the floor in the kitchen would be a good deal more uneven *after* he had relaid it than before ...

The police lost no more time. In Dinham Villa several officers stood around and walked about, carefully scrutinizing the floors in all the rooms. In the kitchen, one of them pointed to some loose flagstones around the hearth. 'We'll have to dig up this lot,' he said. 'After all, we've come this far, so we might as well make a proper job of it.'

The date was 16 March 1892, just thirteen days after the gruesome discovery in Australia 12,000 miles away. Armed with shovels and crow-bars, a squad of officers attacked an area which was less well laid than the remainder of the floor. As they worked, a noisome stench assailed their nostrils. Several young constables vomited uncontrollably. A senior officer sent out for strong cigars, and windows were hurriedly thrown open.

First to be unearthed was the body of a woman wearing

a white nightdress, her long dark hair draped around her shoulders and breast and matted with blood. Her throat had been cut. Then the shocked officers uncovered the bodies of four children. The youngest had been strangled; the other three had had their throats cut. All were dressed in their night-clothes. The bodies were laid neatly side by side in a deep hollow beneath the floor, covered with cement, after which the flagstones which had been removed had been re-laid on top at a noticeably higher level than the rest of the floor.

After the post-mortems on the bodies, police photographs were published, and these brought a swift response. Two brothers, both surnamed Deeming, contacted the police, stating that the woman was the wife of their brother, Frederick Baily Deeming, aged thirty-eight, now in Australia, and the other photographs were those of his four children. The man had married his wife, Marie James of Birkenhead, twelve years previously. 'We thought they were all still living in Liverpool,' one of the brothers said. 'They certainly never lived in London, to our knowledge.'

Cables began to hum between England and Australia. Their man, Frederick Baily Deeming, alias Albert Williams, alias Baron Swanston, was a bigamist and seven-times murderer, and the unfortunate and gullible Kate Roundsfell had been saved in the nick of time from a fate which would have included death ...

While crowds stood in the drizzle in the Rainhill churchyard as the five pathetic victims were buried, Deeming arrived under armed guard in Perth, Western Australia, pending extradition proceedings to Victoria. For ten days his counsel, Richard Haynes, Q.C., fought to stop the extradition order, but failed. Under heavy guard, which included Detective Sergeant Cawsey from Melbourne, Deeming left Perth on the journey by train and ship which was to take him to stand trial in Melbourne.

At country railway stations along the route jeering crowds gathered on the platform to shout abuse and bang on the doors of the coaches with sticks and hoes. In one place a crowd of more than 200 assembled, screaming 'Lynch the bastard!' and 'Cement him!' A scythe shattered the window of the compartment in which Deeming was travelling and an angry mob in ugly mood fought to enter. Police managed to repel the crowd while the guard, seeing the commotion, hastily blew his whistle and the train moved off to hoots of derision from the frustrated would-be lynchers.

Amid howls and catcalls, Deeming arrived in Melbourne on 1 April 1892, and at his preliminary appearance in court he was sent for trial on 22 April at the Supreme Court. He was defended by Mr Alfred Deakin, a brilliant advocate who was later to become a Prime Minister of Australia. Deakin moved for a postponement to allow him time to prepare a defence based upon insanity – his only hope of saving his client's neck. The judge, Mr Justice Hodges, in the light of the hysteria surrounding the trial, made no secret of the fact that he wanted to get it over with as soon as possible. The Press was quite unashamedly whipping up hostile prejudice, unmindful of the effect this could have in preventing Deeming from having a fair trial.

For Deakin to succeed in his insanity plea he had to prove that his client did not know he was doing wrong at the time when he committed the murder, but the doctors the lawyer called to the stand were very little help and even in some cases detrimental to his cause. But the judge refused to grant a postponement and the trial proper commenced. It lasted four days.

Deakin put up a ferocious fight for his client's life, but it was unavailing. Evidence was piled up against Deeming by the prosecutor, Mr Walsh, Q.C., including an unclaimed trunk discovered at a small country railway station in Bairnsdale, Victoria. The trunk contained articles of women's clothing, including a hat which former passengers on board the *Kaiser Wilhelm II* remembered Emily Williams (née Mather) wearing. The key to this trunk was found on Deeming. Mr Walsh also tried to scotch the insanity argument by pointing out that Deeming had told both the ironmonger and the builders' merchant who had made the deliveries to his house at 57 Andrew Street that he wanted the materials to do some concrete work in the back garden. This was not insanity, he said – it was deliberate lying on the part of a guilty man in order to mislead the two men.

By five o'clock in the afternoon of the fourth day the prosecution and the defence had made their final speeches and the judge had given his summing-up, and the jury retired. In three hours and forty minutes they returned, with a verdict of guilty, adding that in their opinion Deeming was sane at the time of committing the crime. When the judge passed sentence of death, Deeming thanked him politely.

'What will happen if I am reprieved?' he asked his counsel. 'You would be extradited to England to stand trial for the Rainhill murders,' he replied. 'In that case,' Deeming answered, 'I'd better get it over and done with here.'

No reprieve was forthcoming; the Privy Council in London refused a stay of execution, and on 23 May 1892 the bogus Baron was executed in Melbourne Gaol. Ten thousand people had gathered outside the prison for the occasion, and as the witnesses to the hanging came out to announce that Frederick Baily Deeming had gone to meet his Maker, a roar of approval went up from the assembled throng as with one voice.

3 The Doctor's Dilemma

The quiet rural lanes of County Cork, in the west of Ireland, echoed with the rhythmic clip-clop of hooves as a pony and trap carried a young girl to a country house where she would take up her new post as governess to the six children of a doctor.

The girl, just twenty, was feeling elated; she had successfully taken a step up the social ladder. From her previous post as a below-stairs nursery maid, she was now to join a household above stairs. But she had studied diligently for three years while still working in order to achieve this improved status. She was now qualified to teach young children the basic educational skills – the three R's – plus cookery, sewing, knitting and embroidery to the four eldest children who were all girls. She was not overly concerned with additional subjects suitable for the little boys – they were only toddlers, one little more than a baby. There would be time to think about them later.

Six children might be quite a handful, but Effie Skinner, their prospective governess, was used to children in her previous post. True, she did not teach them, but she came into contact with them quite often in the course of her duties. She was very fond of children, and they seemed to like her well enough.

The pony drew up at Shandy Hall, the country residence of Dr Philip Cross, who had been an army medical officer in colonial service in India for most of his professional life. He was used to having plenty of servants, and his wife, pale and wraith-like with little interest in anything beyond her brood, had her own personal maid as well as the usual complement of housemaids, cook, stable boys, and so on.

Philip Cross, at sixty-two, was still very much aware of, and susceptible to, feminine attractions, and when Effie Skinner demurely removed her hat and shook out her mane of wavy auburn tresses, his eyes lit up appreciatively. He said very little; it was his wife who had made the choice of governess for his children, and he could not but concur with his wife's choice. A very nice-looking choice indeed, he thought to himself …

Philip Cross was a man of few words, but his taciturnity concealed a multitude of intentions. He would contrive to be out in the stables giving orders to the groom when Effie was taking her charges to see the horses. He would be walking in the gardens, perhaps ostensibly to supervise the gardener, at times when Effie was picnicking with the children under one of the huge oaks in the grounds on a summer afternoon. He would pass her in the hall in the morning as she made her way to the schoolroom. Her very demureness drew him irresistibly. He disliked these forward little city minxes who didn't know their place. And she was a looker, too.

The doctor spent many hours in his study, increasingly unable to concentrate on his medical books. His head was filled with fantasies about Effie Skinner. What was he going to do? It was one thing to sit imagining all kinds of delights, but it was quite another to do anything about it, with his wife and six children in the house. The doctor was in a dilemma indeed. And this man of few words was not the type of person who would rush blindly into a situation beyond his control. He deliberated on the matter for months.

And Effie? She could not fail to be aware of the interest this man had in her. He was a kind and considerate employer, and it was becoming increasingly obvious day by day that his interest in her was going beyond kindness and consideration. She was flattered, as any young girl unversed in the ways of the world would be. She was a simple and unsophisticated country girl, and considered Dr Cross to be a gentleman. After all, did he not live in a big country house with servants and horses and several acres of grounds? Wasn't that supposed to be the mark of a gentleman?

One day Philip Cross passed Effie on the stairs. Her proximity inflamed him – the perfume of her hair, the warmth that radiated from her body. He caught her around the waist, drew her to him and kissed her. Effie did not cry out, or struggle, or slap his face. When he released her, he knew that his attentions had not been unwelcome.

It was but the first of many such encounters – contrived encounters, carefully planned to look like chance ones. As Effie's employer, Philip Cross knew when would be likely times to catch her unawares – or at least seemingly so. His infatuation quickly became an obsession, which he considered was true love. Maybe, after his own fashion, it was. Eventually, after many more weeks of infiltration into her own heart, he declared that he loved her, and he was overjoyed to realize that she felt the same way about him. One afternoon, while his wife was attending a local fair with the children, the two became lovers in deed as well as word.

Philip Cross was so besotted with the slender girl who had entered his life and taken hold of it so completely that he soon began to throw all caution to the winds and become careless. The two were spotted in an embrace by the older children, and it was inevitable that Mrs Cross discovered what was going on under her very nose. She did not scream, or throw a fit of the vapours, or go into hysterics, as many another Victorian wife would have done. Calmly and quietly, she ordered Effie Skinner to pack her belongings and leave – at once. She had the coachman harness the pony, put the girl's luggage in the trap, and bid him convey her to the nearest railway station that same night. 'You can go wherever you like,' Mrs Cross said, 'but do not have the effrontery to ask me for a reference. Here is your month's wages in lieu – that should see you through until you find another job.'

Mrs Cross thought that once she had banished the young woman from her home she had saved her husband from his self-imposed collision course with disaster, rescued her marriage in the nick of time and avoided the scandal of their lives being ruined by a home-breaker. But she was mistaken. She had not reckoned with the love that held Philip Cross in its iron grip. Before the girl had left the premises he had sought her out while his wife was busy bathing the two youngest children, and told her: 'Go to Dublin. Here is some money – go and stay at O'Donnell's Hotel and wait there until I come to you. I will try not to be too long. I have already made the arrangements. Mrs O'Donnell knows you will be coming and has prepared a room for you with all meals provided. I will look after you. You cannot stay in County Cork; the scandal would leak out and I would be ruined. Then there is your reputation to think of. Do not write to me at Shandy Hall ...'

Effie found that Dr Cross was a man of his word. Mrs O'Donnell welcomed her, and she was looked after in the big city. Winter brought not only the snows but also visits by the doctor to his mistress. His wife may have wondered at what business matters required his trips to Dublin with increasing frequency, but, whatever she might have thought, she said nothing. She still had her husband with his medical practice and her home intact. Better not to ask too many questions. Besides, she had no proof that he was not attending medical conventions – other doctors did so all the time.

Meanwhile, Dr Cross was finding the continual travelling about distinctly inconvenient from the standpoint of his obligations to his numerous patients. He really must think of some better way to have his cake and eat it too ... There was really only one way, he thought to himself. Not the ideal solution, of course, but he had no choice.

Mrs Cross suddenly fell sick. She took to her bed, weakened by vomiting and diarrhoea. Her husband prescribed for her, and she gradually recovered. She still felt weak, but chatted amiably about the prospect of being able to go for walks in the fresh air as soon as spring arrived. Long before spring came, however, she suffered a relapse. 'Just a touch of typhoid again,' her husband assured her. 'I'll have Godfrey come in for a second opinion.'

Dr Godfrey was his cousin, newly-qualified and in his early twenties. When he arrived at Shandy Hall he was received patronizingly, as good as told what the patient was suffering from, and told what to do and say. When he asked for specimens of urine and vomit for laboratory examination, he was told that the housemaid had removed them and flushed them down the lavatory. If Dr Godfrey thought it strange that the housemaid would have been allowed into the sickroom where there was a case of the highly-infectious typhoid, he said nothing. After all, he was a very young doctor and anxious to ingratiate himself into the family. Dr Cross was a prominent physician, and getting on a bit, as they say – perhaps at some later stage there might be an opening for Dr Godfrey in a most lucrative practice. He duly diagnosed typhoid. But was it typhoid? Some of the symptoms were a bit odd for typhoid. Still, he wasn't prepared to argue with an experienced ex-army medical officer who had seen service in India. He should know typhoid when he saw it.

Soon after Dr Godfrey had left, the local priest, Fr. Hayes, called, only to be informed that the patient was asleep and was on no account to be disturbed. Typhoid? Fr. Hayes was puzzled. Typhoid was rampant in poor areas where the sanitation left much to be desired. But at Shandy Hall? The house was as clean and healthy as it was possible to be. How could Mrs Cross have possibly contracted typhoid?

A week passed, during which Mrs Cross became gradually weaker and weaker, until at last she gave up the unequal struggle. Mary Buckley, one of the maids, was summoned one morning by loud knocking on the door of the room she shared with another maid. It was the master. 'I need some help,' he said. 'Your mistress has just died.'

As Mary Buckley rose and dressed quickly, she wondered at the cool and matter-of-fact tone of the master's voice. Considering that his wife had just died, he did not sound in the least distraught. It was the same tone of voice in which he would have asked her to fetch the coals.

Dr Cross, after sitting down and writing out a death certificate for Laura Cross, stating that she had died of typhoid, ate a hearty breakfast – even the cook commented on the fact that the bereaved husband had not, apparently, lost his appetite – and then sent Mary Buckley to fetch the undertaker. When he came, he was told to provide for a modest interment in the shortest time possible, and in fact this was carried out at the early hour of 6 a.m. two days later. The date of the funeral was 4 June 1887. Some of the dead woman's friends, who had naturally expected to attend her funeral, were shocked to find the ceremony had already taken place when they arrived. Villagers also commented with a sense of outrage at Philip Cross's unseemly haste, though some pointed out that he had spent most of his adult life in practice in India, where rapid burials were usual owing to the climate. 'It's just what one is used to,' one pointed out.

Laura Cross had hardly been laid to rest when Dr Cross made equally hasty arrangements for a woman to look after his children while he hotfooted it to Dublin, where he intended to stay for a time. In fact, he added, he might even go to England afterwards. He gave no reasons, but the village gossips nodded knowingly and said that it wasn't to attend a medical convention he was going for ...

In Dublin, the girlish dreams of Effie Skinner were at last coming true. She was going to marry the man she loved and, what was more, marrying a gentleman who would make her a lady. She would never need to go out to work and be at the beck and call of anyone; she could wear fine linens, silks and satins, and have a coach and horses at *her* beck and call as well as a cook and maids. The only jammy faces and sticky fingers of children she would ever need to wipe would be those of her own, if the good Lord saw fit to bless her with them. In addition, she would have a ready-made family of six stepchildren. Security and status, as well as love – weren't they what every young girl yearned for?

Philip Cross helped Effie choose the clothes for her wedding trousseau. As he did so, he spoke little of his wife, beyond saying that she had died of typhoid fever. Effie was quite surprised that she could have caught typhoid – just as the parish priest had been – and supposed that perhaps she had touched something that had been contaminated by germs from one of her husband's patients. After a time she ceased to wonder, being utterly absorbed in choosing a veritable dream of a wedding-dress in satin and lace.

Just two weeks after Laura Cross had been buried, the couple took the steamer to England, where Philip Cross and Effie Skinner were married in style at fashionable St James's Church, Piccadilly, in London. When she swept down the aisle on the arm of her adoring husband, she thought that there could not be a happier woman in the whole world. It was just one year since she had arrived at Shandy Hall with just an old black trunk of luggage in a hired pony-and-trap.

The honeymoon was spent in London sightseeing – and the sights certainly made a tremendous impression on the young, simple country girl from County Cork. The shops, the lights, the bustling crowds, the social whirl, left her dizzy with excitement. But, all too soon, the call of duty came, when her husband announced that they would have to return soon to Shandy Hall and his medical practice. Dr Godfrey had been appointed locum, and was finding such a large practice a bit much for his youth and inexperience. Besides, a strange woman was looking after his children. A stepmother they already knew and were fond of was a much better proposition altogether.

So, reluctantly, Effie had to leave behind the delights of the great city and return to the quiet and uneventful life of the Irish countryside. But she was with the husband she loved, which made up for a lot. What she did not reckon with, however, was the chilly reception she received from the villagers, even the servants. Only the children welcomed her with open arms. Neighbours who had been previously in the habit of calling and staying to tea no longer came to the Hall. Tongues wagged, and not just female ones either. There was talk over beer in the taverns, too.

All this came to the attention of Inspector Tyack of the Gardaí (the Irish police) and the implications of some of the opinions he had heard bandied about impelled him to call on the local coroner, who informed him that there had been no post-mortem because a qualified physician had signed the death certificate. When Inspector Tyack asked who that had been, he was told that it had been Dr Cross himself.

'Dr Cross himself!' he exploded. 'That is highly irregular! I shall make some inquiries, and I may well be coming back.'

'I wouldn't be surprised if you do,' the coroner replied.

Tyack called on several people who had been friendly with Dr Cross and his first wife, and the stories they told him had ominous undertones. One family demanded an exhumation. Dr Philip Cross still had a high social standing in the community, mainly on account of his honourable Army career, but Tyack was not a man to let such a thing stand between him and what he considered to be his duty. He applied to the local magistrate for an exhumation order, and handed it to the coroner with a request that an inquest be held.

Within a few hours the mortal remains of Laura Cross had been exhumed and taken to the local mortuary, where the pathologist started work. His findings would either scotch the rumours that were being bandied about, or they would prove that she had died of typhoid after all, unlikely though it seemed in a place like Shandy Hall.

At the inquest, Philip Cross attended, sitting alone and aloof and showing no sign of the turmoil within him. Effie did not attend. His only comment was to express restrained anger and repugnance at the invasion of his former wife's final resting-place. But there were no sensational developments; Inspector Tyack was too shrewd a policeman to move without proven knowledge of the truth, and for that he must await the post-mortem results. The inquest was formally adjourned until a date set by the coroner which would allow the pathologist time to complete his work.

At home, Philip Cross was moody and withdrawn. Even Effie was unable to penetrate the dark clouds that enveloped his mind. She felt a growing presentiment of disaster, but could not put a name to it. She kept her fears to herself, valiantly hiding her unease so as not to add to her husband's burden – the burden of the secret he could not share with her.

The day before the inquest was resumed, Inspector Tyack went to Shandy Hall, and when he left he was accompanied by Philip Cross. The doctor was taken to Cork, and charged with the murder of Laura Cross. The next day, at the inquest, the pathologist gave evidence that she had died, not from typhoid, but from arsenic poisoning.

The doctor was kept in custody in Cork until the next Munster Assizes on 14 December 1887. More evidence was produced to incriminate the man who had murdered one woman for the love of another. A witness was produced in the form of a chemist who had sold pure arsenic to a man answering to the description of the prisoner in the dock, and it was also trenchantly pointed out to the jury that a doctor who had spent as long in practice in India as Philip Cross had done could not possibly be mistaken as to the symptoms of typhoid fever, so it could be presumed that he had lied for reasons best known to himself.

The pathologist produced evidence to prove that the amount of arsenic present in Laura Cross's remains was 3.2 grains – a residual quantity which would have been the result of feeding the victim arsenic systematically for several months. The chemist who had sold it stated that the customer had signed the poisons register as 'C. Osborne, Farmer, of Sligo' and wanted it for a sheep-dip.

Despite the verdict being a foregone conclusion, the trial lasted for four days, Cross's counsel putting up a valiant fight, but all his efforts proved unavailing, and Mr Justice Murphy sentenced the doctor to death. Asked if he had anything to say, the prisoner replied simply, 'My lord, it was not me.'

On 10 January 1888 the doctor, a broken man, his hair turned white since his imprisonment, was led from the condemned cell to the gallows. He had made the ultimate sacrifice for the woman he loved, and now he had to pay the ultimate price.

4   A Slight Misunderstanding

The entire direction of a person's life may sometimes be changed by a trivial misunderstanding. The time of an appointment may be misheard; the place for a meeting may be mistaken for the name of another place. It was just such a slight misunderstanding on the part of a vivacious young girl of seventeen that made all the difference in the world – the difference between life and death.

Bronwyn Richardson, a blue-eyed, blonde supermarket check-out girl, lived with her brother in Plummer Street, Albury, in the Australian state of New South Wales. She worked at Cole's New World Supermarket, not far from their flat.

In October 1973 a dance was being held in Coreen, a town some twenty or so miles from Albury, and Bronwyn was looking forward to attending, escorted by her boyfriend Michael O'Bryan. He was twenty-three, the son of a farmer from Drysdale, a couple of miles from Coreen, where the dance was being held.

Michael was having some mechanical trouble with the old car he had recently purchased, and he could not use it until repairs had been carried out. So he arranged with a friend, Charles Kerr, to meet Bronwyn after she finished work on the Friday night and drive her to the dance in Coreen.

At the appointed time Bronwyn moved across the street from Cole's New World to wait for Charles outside St Patrick's Presbytery which, like Cole's, was in Smollett Street. From this vantage-point she had a much better view, being able to see not only anyone who went to the supermarket entrance but also cars approaching from any direction. There was a streetlight in the centre of the road.

Although she did not know what kind of car Charles would be driving, she did of course know him. She was not a girl to accept a ride from a complete stranger, and never hitched, so she could not afford to miss her lift with Charles. She had been waiting now for more than an hour, and was wondering what had happened to him. She had some disappointing news for him, too: the girlfriend she had tried to persuade to come with her to the dance as a partner for Charles was unable to go owing to a prior engagement. She had tried one or two of her other work-mates, but all were 'booked'.

Aha! At last – here was a car coming that was slowing as it approached her. But it was a woman driving, who gave Bronwyn a curious glance, then picked up speed and drove on. Where *was* Charles?

At about the same time as Bronwyn would have been peering hopefully into the passing car, Charles had arrived at her flat in Plummer Street. Her brother Gary was out, and there was no reply to his knock at the door of the darkened apartment. Charles asked one or two of the nearest neighbours whether they had seen Bronwyn, but no one had seen her since she had left for work early that morning. Next, Charles tried Cole's New World Supermarket; this too was in darkness. He drove around the area for a while, hoping he might spot her in the street. He began to feel a little uneasy; if anything had happened to Bronwyn it would be his fault for not picking her up on time. He felt a certain responsibility to his friend Michael, too. But he shrugged off any notion that something untoward had overtaken the girl; that kind of thing happened in the big cities, not a little town like Albury …

Eventually he came to the conclusion that a colleague from the supermarket must have driven Bronwyn to Coreen after he had missed her at the appointed time. By now it was 8.15 – too late to go to the dance. Bronwyn and Michael were probably there anyway by now. Charles picked up a Chinese take-away meal, and drove home. He still could not entirely dismiss the niggling uneasiness at the back of his mind …

At about this time, Bronwyn's parents, Stan and Noeline Richardson, who lived in Guy Street in the small

A Slight Misunderstanding

town of Corowa, 24 miles from Albury, were driving towards Albury to visit Stan's sister. Driving along the Howlong Road, they passed a turning called Horsfall Lane, a mile or two before coming into Albury. A car was parked with its lights on near this turning, which led to a popular fishing spot known as Four Mile Reserve. Mrs Richardson remarked casually that it was a bit late for someone to be fishing.

In Albury the Richardsons stayed in their relatives' home until the early hours, when they bid their farewell and headed back home, arriving at about 3 a.m. The car was gone when they passed the Horsfall Lane turning on the return journey.

Meanwhile, Michael O'Bryan was told by a friend that Charles Kerr had missed Bronwyn somehow in Albury, and that Charles had concluded that Bronwyn had made her own way to Coreen, probably with a supermarket colleague who had a car. Michael and his pal went into the dance-hall and looked for the girl, but she was nowhere to be found. For the next hour the two of them wandered around the crowded, smoky ballroom, but Bronwyn did not show up. Finally, he came to the conclusion that she had felt unwell and had gone to her parents' home instead, but when he tried to ring them there was no reply. Eventually he was driven home in his friend's car. His parents had not heard from her either. He just did not know what to think. Not at his home, not at her parents' home, not at her own place, not at the dance-hall. Where could she be?

By mid-morning the next day, Saturday, with no news of the missing girl, it was decided to report her disappearance to the police in Albury. It was quite out of character for Bronwyn just to drop out of sight without a word to anybody; she was not a free-wheeling hippie who would take off as the mood took her, but a hard-working girl who kept in touch with her family and was known to be reliable and responsible.

When the Richardsons, accompanied by Michael O'Bryan, arrived at the police headquarters in Albury, their fears were confirmed. A woman had found and handed in about two hours previously a woman's black patent shoe and a black vinyl handbag, which she had picked up near St Patrick's Presbytery the previous night at about 10 p.m. The Richardsons recognized the items at once as belonging to their daughter. The bag contained Bronwyn's provisional driving licence, her powder compact, lipstick and other cosmetics, and her unopened wage-packet containing $37.22. The police, however, emphasized that there was no reason to suspect foul play just because a handbag had been handed in; anyone could drop or lose a handbag. But a shoe, Mrs Richardson pointed out: women just do not go around dropping or losing their shoes! The police agreed, somewhat reluctantly, that perhaps it would be a good idea to institute a search after all ...

The understaffed small-town police-force may at first have considered that the missing girl had gone off somewhere without telling anybody, and that the lost items handed in were just that and no more. But they were soon to change their minds, and to concede that the parents had been right after all. A search was made throughout the town, extending outwards into the rural areas and along the banks of the Murray River, and at dawn the next morning Bronwyn's body was discovered in the river, caught up in vegetation at a spot known as Horseshoe Bend – a spot only a few hundred yards from the place where the Richardsons had seen the parked car on the Friday night.

A post-mortem showed that Bronwyn had been savagely raped, strangled and thrown unconscious into the river to drown. Her black flared jeans had been tied round her ankles, and her purple blouse and sweater were bunched up around her neck. There was no sign of her underclothes. She had been a virgin prior to the rape.

Superintendent F.L. Kiernan, the head of police for the district in which the body was found, took charge of the investigation. Soon twelve detectives were working on the case, in sharp contrast to the desultory manner in which the search had been started. A search of the river-bank revealed Bronwyn's wrist-watch about a hundred yards from where her body was found. It had stopped at 7.26.

An appeal was made for the mystery woman car driver

to come forward in person – she had telephoned the police to say she thought she had seen the girl apparently waiting for someone on the Friday night, but had not given her name. She was Mrs Denise Prochazka, who had attended an evening service, leaving the church at about 6.45 p.m., seeing Bronwyn moments later as she was driving home. At 7.05 another woman, Vera Williams, was waiting just a few yards from the scene outside the doors of the bingo hall, which was due to open. A car drove past, and she thought she saw two men struggling with a woman inside. She thought they were just young people skylarking about. Police believed that the parked car seen by the Richardsons may have contained the man or men who murdered Bronwyn. It would appear, therefore, that the entire operation – kidnapping, rape and murder – took place in the space of thirty minutes.

Just thirty minutes was all it took to abduct a young girl off the street, probably by force, during which she dropped her handbag and a shoe as she struggled, and consign her to a watery grave, apparently while she was still alive, after a ferocious criminal assault. And all because Charles Kerr had understood from Michael O'Bryan that Bronwyn would be waiting at her flat in Plummer Street for him to pick her up, whereas Bronwyn had understood that Charles would pick her up outside the supermarket after it closed. Truly a person's destiny may depend on a few spoken words, a trivial misunderstanding.

5 The Toy Soldier

Still in New South Wales, Australia, we now go back in time to 1931 when two policemen paid the ultimate price of the pent-up frustrations of a man whose mind was unhinged because he thought he had been given a raw deal. But first let us take a look at his background and trace the path that led him to the point where he literally went over the edge.

John Thomas Kennedy's favourite occupation as a small boy was to don a military-style hat made out of newspaper and brandish a wooden sword or a toy rifle, parading to and fro in front of all the neighbours. As he grew up, his obsession never left him, and he took pride in his strong physique and robust health. As a teenager he joined the young cadets' corps in the militia, but his disappointment knew no bounds when he developed painful varicose veins in his legs and was forced to resign. This setback depressed him considerably at the time, but eventually he learned to accept the inevitable.

When the First World War started in 1914, John Kennedy, at twenty-six, was living in the Sydney suburb of Waverley with his widowed mother, to whom he was devoted, and his sisters. He was a skilled colour printer earning the then considerable sum of twenty-four dollars a week, but the prospect of joining the army and fighting in the war seized him with urgency, although he knew that a soldier's pay would be meagre indeed compared with his wages in the printing-shop. Rushing to enlist, he was flatly rejected at the medical examination on account of his varicose veins. The decision struck him like a physical blow.

As the war progressed and more and more of Australia's

young men answered the call to the colours, few around him understood completely the depth of John Kennedy's dismay and despondency. He became increasingly self-conscious, especially when neighbours commented on his apparent strength and manliness. After all, his varicose veins were hidden by his clothes. In 1916 he again tried to enlist and was again rejected. A few weeks later he found an envelope addressed to him in the mail, written in a delicate feminine hand. Inside there was no letter – just a white feather, symbol of cowardice. His mother and sisters made light of the incident, telling him to ignore what was just the rude joke of an ignorant person. But to John it was a profound insult from which he never really recovered.

In 1919 his mother died – another shattering blow. After the funeral, the memories became too much for him and he decided to move to Melbourne. He managed to find work, but his inability to make friends and his inevitable loneliness drove him back to Sydney, which was at least familiar to him. This time he did not live at home with his sisters but settled in a cottage in Lawson Street in the suburb of Waverley. Although he soon found a good job and was not short of money, he furnished the cottage with only the barest of necessities, and became so introverted that even his sisters were not made welcome.

In his job in the printing department of a newspaper, he kept himself aloof from his work-mates, but was considered to be a conscientious employee. Around his home in Lawson Street he soon became known as an eccentric. He had taken up the flute, which he did play well but unfortunately for his neighbours he preferred to practise in the small hours of the morning. He also disturbed their sleep with the rhythmic thump of hobnailed boots as he marched back and forth across the bare floorboards, shouting out commands in a loud voice. Many believed that he was a returned soldier suffering from shellshock.

Even when he was engaged in target practice in his backyard with a .22, no one considered him dangerous, just a harmless fanatic, known as 'the mad general' or 'Mad Kennedy'. Neighbourhood boys came to watch his antics through holes in the fence, and sometimes he would spin them yarns of imagined military exploits in the war.

Kennedy's mental obsessions seemed to reach a peak in 1931. He became more and more introspective, rarely going out and staying indoors in the cottage which, to him, had become a military barracks. He spent the New Year holiday of that year writing poetry and composing military music.

On Saturday, 3 January, he decided he must go out as he wanted some cigarettes. Armed with a rifle and with a Bowie knife in his belt, he marched with soldierly strides along Ebley Street until he reached Bondi Junction. Few, however, took much notice of the tall figure with the rifle slung over his shoulder and wearing a military-style uniform. The Junction was a very busy area on a Saturday morning, and people were hurrying about their business.

John entered a tobacconist's and imperiously ordered cigarettes. After they had been handed to him, he turned smartly on his heel and made to walk out of the shop. The proprietor reached the door before him to remind him that he had not paid for them.

'You can charge them to the government,' Kennedy said.

'I can't do that, sir,' the proprietor replied. 'I'm afraid you'll have to pay for them yourself.'

'I'll have this shop shut up and put you before a firing squad!' barked Kennedy in his best parade-ground voice. And with these words he flung the cigarettes on the floor between them.

The tobacconist realized that the man was mentally unbalanced, and considered that he might be dangerous, seeing the rifle and the Bowie knife. He followed Kennedy out and crossed the road to the policeman on point-duty. Constable Norman Allen, seeing the armed man pushing his way through the crowds, with complete disregard for his own safety left his traffic spot and sprinted after the military figure. Catching up with him about 150 yards further along the street, he tapped him lightly on the shoulder. 'I think you'd better give me that rifle,' he said quietly.

To John Kennedy, the sight of a uniformed policeman was synonymous with an enemy to be repulsed. He swung round, levelled the rifle and fired into the constable's chest at point-blank range. As the officer slumped to the ground, Kennedy fired two more rounds into his body. The crowds were stunned with horror as they saw the policeman collapse bleeding against a wall.

In the crowd was Steve Robinson, a well-known Sydney football player. 'Give me his gun, quick!' he cried. Someone took the dying constable's revolver from its holster and handed it to Robinson. He ran after Kennedy, who continued on his way without looking round after the shooting. A plain-clothes detective named McGill happened to be passing in a bus and witnessed the shooting. Jumping off the bus, he too sprinted after Kennedy. Hearing footsteps behind him, Kennedy swung round and pointed his rifle straight at his pursuers.

'Get back!' he shouted. 'Can't you see I'm exercising the law'.

McGill dived for cover into a telephone box which was conveniently at hand, and called for police reinforcements. Then he ran to catch up with Steve Robinson, who had found that Constable Allen's revolver had jammed. McGill hastily cleared the mechanism and the two men then continued after Kennedy as he now approached his home in Lawson Street.

Police reinforcements arrived very shortly. Constable Ernest Andrews, a young Englishman recently arrived in Australia, was on a Bondi tram with his companion Constable Denholme when they saw the disturbance at the Junction. Although off-duty (they had been heading for the beach), they did not hesitate when they saw the body of Constable Norman Allen. Alighting from the tram, they turned into Ebley Street in hot pursuit of the fugitive. Kennedy had by now reached his home in Lawson Street, ignoring warnings from Detective McGill to surrender his weapon. Kennedy's answer was to swing round and point it at his pursuers, who ducked for cover. Hearing the commotion, several neighbours were standing in their doorways. 'It's the Mad General!' they said. 'He's really gone off his rocker this time, no doubt about it!'

'The Mad General' was by now safely inside his house, and when McGill and Steve Robinson tried the front door they found it locked. Wisely, they decided to await the arrival of the squad cars. The two off-duty constables, still carrying their beach towels and of course unarmed, decided to try the back door and ran along the alley which separated Kennedy's house from that of his neighbour. A woman's voice could be heard calling out, 'Don't go in there! He's raving mad!'

Constable Andrews was not to be discouraged. The vision of his colleague and friend Norman Allen, propped bleeding against the wall, still swam before his eyes. Grabbing a paling from the fence which he ripped out with the superhuman strength born of desperation, he ran to the back door of the cottage, which was unlocked. As he entered the darkened kitchen, the tall figure of the Mad General stood framed in the doorway, ready to repulse the enemy. 'Get back!' he shouted. But Andrews moved forwards towards him. Kennedy fired two shots; he could hardly have missed. Andrews stumbled, already mortally wounded, but Kennedy leaped forward and dealt him a final blow with his Bowie knife.

The men in front of the house, hearing the shots and throwing all caution to the winds, tried to crash the front door open, but it would not budge. More police reinforcements now arrived, and Constable Johnson drew his revolver and fired at the leaded lights on either side of the door. Through the gap in the shattered glass they could see Kennedy brandishing his rifle menacingly. Ducking hastily, Johnson fired again; this time the bullet hit Kennedy in the stomach. Uttering a scream of rage and pain, Kennedy dropped his weapons and staggered into a ground floor room used as a bedroom, clutching his stomach in agony. As he tried to rise to his feet a pair of handcuffs was snapped on his wrists. Someone had telephoned for an ambulance, and the crowd which had assembled saw Kennedy carried out of the house on a stretcher to be taken to St Vincent's Hospital, where he died a few hours later, still babbling incoherently about the enemy.

In the cottage, police found, among all the poetry and

music scores, hundreds of rounds of ammunition and enough food stocks for a prolonged siege. There was also a diary, with detailed entries, some very disjointed, indicating Kennedy's acute paranoia. In some ways I feel this is one of the most poignant cases in this book. Had Kennedy lived today, it is pretty certain that he could have sought treatment for his varicose veins, after which he could have been accepted into the army where his obsession with war and fighting could have been channelled into a satisfying outlet that would not have left two brave constables lying dead in the prime of their youth.

The policemen's funeral was the biggest ever seen in Sydney. Thousands lined the streets to pay tribute to the courage of Constables Norman Allen and Ernest Andrews, who laid down their lives in the line of duty.

6 The Pillbox Murder

'Can I go out to play, Ma?' asked Andrew Bonnick, a fourteen-year-old schoolboy who lived with his parents at The Cot, a little cottage in the seaside village of Gileston, near Barry in Glamorganshire, Wales. It was Thursday, 29 December 1960, and the children had not yet, of course, returned to school after the Christmas holidays.

'Yes, you can go – provided you don't stay out too long,' his mother agreed with some reluctance as she prepared the family's tea in the tiny kitchen. 'Don't forget – you be back by four o'clock,' she continued, raising her voice slightly as Andrew hurried out of the back door, down the garden path, and headed for the beach just under a mile away.

Andrew's father, a plant attendant at the Central Electricity Generating Board, was on night duty over this holiday period, and that afternoon after lunch he left the house to collect his wages and do some shopping in nearby St Athan. Andrew had wanted to accompany him to the shops so that he could spend some of his Christmas present money, but his father had persuaded him to postpone his shopping trip until the following day.

As Andrew crossed the field which lay beyond the garden gate to reach the beach he was watched by his mother and his three sisters, Joyce, twelve, Aileen, six, and baby Moira, three, until he was out of sight. Then Mrs Bonnick returned to her task of preparing high tea for her family.

It was later learned that at about 2.30 p.m. Andrew met two of his school-friends, Brian Dunn, who was also fourteen, and Geoffrey Wilmott, a year younger, both of whom lived in St Athan. The three played together by the edge of the sea for a while, then walked along the beach talking, as boys do, of their various interests and hobbies. Soon after three o'clock Andrew left his companions, saying that his mother would be expecting him home for his tea at four o'clock. The last his two companions saw of him was as he walked slowly in the direction of the old Second World War concrete pillboxes and defence blocks which still stood at the beachhead, idly picking up pebbles and seeing how far he could throw them into the sea.

They also noticed a young man, a stranger to them, walking in the same direction that Andrew was taking. About twenty minutes later they noticed him again, this time apparently peeping out at them from behind the concrete defence blocks. The stranger continued to watch them for several minutes in this way; it was most uncanny how the chap's eyes seemed to be fixed rigidly upon them. 'What's that fellow staring at us like that for?' remarked Brian to his companion.

'I dunno. Let's go home – there's nothing to do here,' replied Geoffrey as they left the beach and trudged towards St Athan. 'At least at home we can watch the telly.'

When Andrew's father arrived home from work soon after 3.30, he told his wife that he would nip up to the beach to collect driftwood for the fire. Mrs Bonnick told him that since Andrew was already at the beach he might as well bring him back with him, which would at least ensure that the boy would not be late for his tea. Her husband agreed that this was a good idea.

A few minutes after Albert Bonnick had left the house, a young fellow spoke to Andrew's three sisters, who were playing in the garden, over the hedge. He asked Joyce, the eldest, whether their mother was in. Joyce was alarmed by the stranger's appearance: his clothing was dishevelled as though he had been in a fight, his hair was, as Joyce put it, 'all messed up', and there were smears of blood on his face and hands. Joyce ran into the house calling for her mother, followed closely by the other two little girls.

Mrs Bonnick, telling the children to stay in the house, went out into the garden. The stranger was very agitated. 'I've found a boy in one of them air-raid shelters up the beach,' he stammered. 'He looks pretty badly knocked about, like he has been beaten up, with a lot of blood an' all that.'

Mrs Bonnick, by now thoroughly alarmed, told him to stay there while she fetched her coat. Enjoining the children to remain in the house until she or their father returned, she hastily grabbed her winter coat and hurried out of the house towards the beach, accompanied by the nervous stranger. As they reached the beach Mrs Bonnick could see her husband just as he was about to enter the middle one of three wartime pillboxes. She could see no sign of her son. As fear mounted in her, her breath came in laboured gasps. 'O God,' she prayed aloud, 'it can't be Andrew – it can't be! Nothing could have happened to him ...'

As he revealed later, Albert Bonnick, as he entered the pillbox, could just make out, in the gloomy interior, the prone form of a boy on the ground, bleeding profusely from fearful head wounds and extensive facial injuries, but it was not until he saw the boy's clothing that he recognized the victim as his own son. With the assistance of the stranger, who by now had joined him, leaving the apprehensive Mrs Bonnick standing a little distance away, Bonnick carried Andrew outside. It was seen that the boy's jeans were at half-mast and his underpants round his knees, although his leather belt was still round his waist. The two men laid him on the shingle and covered him with his father's jacket and pullover and the stranger's donkey jacket, and while one of the two men stayed with the stricken boy the other ran to the nearest public telephone. Soon an ambulance arrived from St Athan, and Andrew was taken to the RAF Hospital, where a team of doctors fought vainly to save the boy's life. At 8.30 p.m. on the same night he died from shock and haemorrhage caused by multiple head injuries.

A heavy notched stick found nearby was proved to be the murder weapon, as on later examination by forensic experts it was found to be covered with blood of the same group as the victim's, to which hairs adhered which matched those of the dead boy.

The stranger was twenty-year-old Malcolm Keith Williams, a fitter's mate, who worked at the power station at Aberthaw, where his father was also employed as a labourer. One of nine children, he lived with his parents in a dilapidated cottage in the Rhondda called Mountain View, in the village of Llwynpia.

Detective Inspector David Davies, from Ton Pentre police-station, arrived at the Williams home at 9.10 p.m. that evening, where he found Malcolm finishing his supper. Malcolm agreed to accompany the officer to the police-station to make a statement, and he was to be interviewed by Detective Chief Superintendent Tom Williams, the chief of the local CID. He, however, was delayed by the post-mortem on the dead boy, which was taking place that same night: criminal investigation moves no less swiftly in Wales than elsewhere. Malcolm Williams and his father, who had accompanied him to the police-station, were given cups of tea, and they did not object to remaining at the police station until the arrival of the superintendent; in fact Malcolm slept, and did not awaken until 5 a.m. the next morning, when he was interviewed.

Chief Superintendent Williams had been on duty for a very long stretch. Throughout the day of the murder he had been on duty and on hearing of the death of the victim he drove to the hospital at St Athan. Late that same evening, accompanied by Inspector D. Austin and Detective Sergeant Howard Evans, he made his way on foot to the pillbox which stood on the lonely beachhead, in the driving rain and near gale-force wind of a dark and stormy December night. The pillbox was situated a mile and a half from the nearest point to which a car could be driven, and the three men had to scramble over slimy, seaweed-encrusted boulders to reach the site. With the help of heavy lighting equipment which had to be carried over the rocks and shingle, Superintendent Williams and his assistants worked on their hands and knees in the pillbox searching for clues, however slight, among the driftwood, stones and other débris, and afterwards looked for any further possible clues on the surrounding beach, often slipping on the wet seaweed.

By the early hours of the following morning the Superintendent was at the hospital once more, this time for the post-mortem on the dead boy, from which he went straight to the police-station at Ton Pentre to interview the suspect. By the time the young man's statement had been taken it was 8.30 a.m., yet three hours later the indefatigable Superintendent was back at the pillbox in daylight, this time with forensic experts from Cardiff. He was still on duty two days later when he was suddenly taken ill, and it was at this point that Detective Superintendent (now ex-Detective Assistant Commissioner, retired) John du Rose, of Scotland Yard's Murder Squad, was called in, on New Year's Eve.

In his statement taken in the early hours of December 30, Malcolm Williams had said that he had been at work in the usual way on the previous day, and that at 12.45 he had lunch in the canteen, after which he had gone on to the beach for a short walk, returning to work at 1.45 when he heard the hooter. He continued working until three o'clock, when he again visited the canteen, staying there until twenty to four. Then, his statement continued, he went on to the beach again, this time 'to collect wood for drying out the pipes', apparently referring to one of his duties which was to clean and dry out the inside of a number of metal pipes at the plant. He then stated that, having collected some wood, he put it into the pillbox to keep it dry for use the following day, and it was then that he found Andrew Bonnick lying there.

On investigation, this statement was found to be a complete fabrication in almost every particular. Both the suspect's father and another power station labourer named Trevor Davis asserted categorically that Malcolm Williams was not in the canteen at lunchtime; it was in fact established that he had lunch in a cafe in St Athan called the Stratford Cafe between 1 and 2 p.m., where he was served with fish and chips and three cups of coffee by the waitress, a Mrs Edna Buffett, who also deposed to having seen him in the cafe on a number of previous occasions, usually on weekday lunch-times. Evidently the canteen at work was not much to his liking.

The suspect's story of 'collecting wood to dry out the pipes' was a tissue of lies from start to finish. The management stated that it was contrary to CEGB regulations to dry out pipes in that way and, furthermore, on 28 December (the day before the murder) Williams had been directed to leave his work in the pipe department and work in the turbine house until further notice, so he was not concerned with pipe work on the day in question. In any case, even if he had been, he could have found plenty of scrap wood in the yard without needing to walk two miles for its collection, and the story of 'leaving it to dry in the pillbox' was patently absurd.

It was also discovered by the police who were so painstakingly investigating the case that soon after two o'clock Williams had spoken to a local schoolgirl, thirteen-year-old Sandra Crick, as she sat on a form by the side of the road leading to Gileston Village. She said that the man, who was a complete stranger, was 'very nervous like, and sort of jumpy and talking very queer like', and as she found his manner disturbing she rose from her seat and ran all the way home, where she told her mother of the incident. When, on 31 December, she saw Williams's photograph in the local evening newspaper, she recognized him immediately and told her mother that he was the man. Sandra Crick's story of her meeting with Williams was confirmed by two of her friends, Christine and Joy Adamson, sisters aged fifteen and thirteen respectively, who both saw her talking to Williams at the time in question and then saw her suddenly leave her seat and run in the direction of her home, and Christine stated that she later noticed the man walking towards the beach.

At 5.30 p.m. on the day of the murder Williams returned to the Stratford café. Mrs Buffett was not there, but the proprietress, a Mrs Hetta Harries, and her niece, Miss Betty Phillips, were on the premises. Both recognized him as the same man whom Mrs Buffett had served at lunch-time on the same day. Williams now seemed very upset and agitated, and Mrs Harries noticed that he had some blood smears on his face and also on one hand. On asking him what had happened to him, he told her that he had 'found a boy in one of them pillboxes up the beach with his head bashed in'. He then asked Mrs Harries to allow him to use her bathroom to wash himself, which she did, and when he returned downstairs she asked him for

The Pillbox Murder

his name and address. He gave her his correct particulars and made no attempt at evasion.

The clothing Williams had worn on the day of the murder, on being examined by Mr Brian Morgan, Senior Scientific Officer at Cardiff Forensic Science Laboratory, was found to be excessively bloodstained, both on the jacket and on the left leg of his jeans. There were several blood spots as well as some large drops on the jacket, and similar spots on the bottom of each trouser leg, indicating that the garments had been in the path of a spray of blood, and thus consistent with having been worn by the victim's attacker. Blue and purple fibres taken from under the dead boy's fingernails also matched fibres from Williams's jacket, indicating that the boy had put up a strenuous resistance.

It was also discovered that Williams had a background history of sexual offences against young children. He had been in trouble with the police on a number of occasions, and at twelve years of age he had been taken into care and sent to a children's home on account of unsatisfactory home conditions. He absconded from the home several times and was eventually sent to an approved school, after a conviction for breaking and entering and theft from a factory. After his release there were various further convictions for theft and he served two terms at Borstal, which he had left only six weeks before the murder. Furthermore, at the approved school he had indulged in homosexual offences against younger boys. In a statement he made to the juvenile court he admitted offences against both younger boys and little girls at various times.

From all appearances, it would seem that Williams had lured Andrew Bonnick into the pillbox on some pretext or another with the intention of committing sodomy, and that when the boy realized this and resisted, Williams's temper was inflamed and in his rage at being frustrated he grabbed the nearest available blunt instrument – in this case, a heavy stick – and crashed it down upon the unfortunate victim's head. The facial injuries may well have been caused by being punched in the eye, possibly when Andrew had told his attacker during the struggle that he would tell his parents – at least, that is the view of one of the police-officers engaged on the case. The post-mortem showed no signs of anal penetration, so it may be assumed that the fatal struggle ensued before Williams's intention could be realised.

It seems to be a somewhat amazing coincidence that at the same time that Williams must have been leaving the pillbox after the crime, the boy's father was leaving his own home for the beach in search of firewood, and also that Williams made his way to the boy's own home, which was the only cottage in sight, as a feeble attempt at an alibi.

Williams was charged with the murder of Andrew Bonnick, and after his initial appearance at Cowbridge Magistrates' Court on 26 January 1961 he was sent for trial at the Glamorganshire Assizes on 27 March of the same year. The trial, presided over by Mr Justice Ashworth, lasted two days. The accused pleaded not guilty, and at no time did he ever display any sign of regret for his actions, or remorse at the death of his victim. In fact he alleged that he had seen 'two boys' near the pillbox who could have committed the crime, and even went to such lengths as to infer that the boy's own father could have killed him. The jury were out for only forty-five minutes before returning a verdict of guilty of murder, and Williams was sentenced to life imprisonment. The Court of Criminal Appeal later refused him leave to appeal.

The pillbox of death no longer stands on that lonely beachhead on the Glamorgan coast. The inhabitants of Gileston and St Athan petitioned the local council for its removal; they wanted no reminder of the violent tragedy that had shattered their peaceful existence. Now only sea-birds wheel above the bare rocks and shingle of Gileston beach, and the concrete monstrosities with their grim memories have been swept away.

7 Hospital of Horror

Children are, as we have seen in the last chapter, vulnerable to strangers even in a public place in broad daylight. The younger the child, the more vulnerable he or she will be. It can readily be imagined that if a young child is, unwisely, allowed to be out unaccompanied after dark, the chances of assault or abduction are immeasurably increased. Incredible as it may seem, however, a young child, not yet four years of age, was abducted from the children's ward of a hospital in 1948, and taken into the hospital grounds, where she was killed after being savagely raped. Nurses were on duty at the time. Who could have possibly imagined that a child was not even safe in a children's hospital ward?

On 15 May 1948 the hush of night had descended on Ward C.3 at Queen's Park Hospital in Blackburn, Lancashire. All the lights had been dimmed except for the small lamp on the night nurse's table; a pile of books, a pad and ballpoint pen and a ruler were evidence of the fact that the staff nurse used her night duty time, when she was not actively engaged in attending to the needs of her patients, in studying for one of the higher nursing examinations. Her ambition was to become eventually a Ward Sister.

At the other end of the long, darkened ward from the now empty table, Night Staff Nurse Gwendolyn Humphries was busy in the little kitchen adjoining the ward preparing six breakfast trays for the morning. These were for the six tiny occupants of Ward C.3, who were all under five years of age; the kitchen adjoined this ward, but Staff Nurse Humphries also had to patrol the adjoining Ward C.4, another children's ward, during the night and generally keep an eye on things until relieved at 6 a.m. by the arrival of the day staff.

Shortly after midnight, a few minutes into 15 May, Nurse Humphries left the kitchen and made a round of both wards; all the little patients were sleeping soundly in their cots. She returned to the kitchen and continued with her breakfast tray preparations. One or two needed special diets. After a few moments she thought she heard one of the children in C.3 call out, but on going to investigate all were sound asleep. It was not unusual for a child to call out in his or her sleep, especially when in unfamiliar surroundings.

The trays now ready, Nurse Humphries went to check Ward C.4, and she was just returning to C.3 when she noticed that the porch door, which she knew had a faulty catch, was swinging open. She closed it, but did not attach any significance to the matter, as a breeze would often blow open the door at any time. She went back to the kitchen to wash the dishes and then to her night table at the other end of the ward to do some studying in the peace and quiet. It was twenty past one.

On leaving the kitchen and entering C.3 she noticed immediately that one of the cots was empty, the bedclothes thrown back. The child who should have been sound asleep there was June Anne Devaney, not quite four years of age, who had been admitted ten days earlier with a touch of mild pneumonia. Fortunately she had not been seriously ill, and in fact had made such a good recovery that she was due for discharge the next day.

Nurse Humphries observed that the drop side of the cot was still in its raised position, which meant that the child herself could not have clambered out but that someone must have lifted her out. In any case, if June had attempted to climb out of her cot Nurse Humphries would have heard noises and gone at once to investigate. Whoever had taken June from her cot had been completely silent. Looking at the floor by the side of the cot, the sharp-eyed nurse also noticed what appeared to be the imprint of a man's bare feet, and under the cot itself was a sterile water-bottle – known as a Winchester bottle – which had most certainly not been there when she

Hospital of Horror

checked the ward on her last round of inspection. All these bottles were kept standing upright on a trolley at the opposite end of the ward.

Nurse Humphries wasted no time in raising the alarm. All the night staff that it was possible to release from ward duty took torches and searched the extensive grounds – the hospital stood in seventy acres – for more than half an hour without finding any trace of the missing child, and the police were then called. Within minutes they arrived and, with the aid of more powerful lighting equipment, searched the grounds until, at 3.17 a.m., they came upon the ravaged body of June Anne Devaney, lying face downwards in the long grass by the wall which enclosed the grounds. She had been killed by her murderer having swung her by the legs and brutally dashed her head against the wall. She had been savagely raped, and in addition her body had been horrendously mutilated by deep teeth marks embedded in the buttocks. Her blood-soaked hospital nightgown had been ripped to shreds.

Forty-three minutes after the finding of the body, Chief Inspector John Capstick of the Yard's Murder Squad had his night's sleep cut short by the ringing of the telephone. The Chief Constable of Lancashire, Sir Archibald Hordern, and the Chief Constable of Blackburn, Mr C.G. Looms, had reported the murder to the Commissioner of the Metropolitan Police, and, when the 6.20 a.m. train drew out of Euston, Capstick, with Detective Sergeant John Stoneman, was already on his way to find the killer of June Anne Devaney.

On their arrival in Blackburn, Chief Inspector Capstick and his assistant found the hospital grounds already sealed off and an intensive search by local police-officers in progress. Daylight now enabled a more thorough inch-by-inch search to be made, despite a light drizzle. The Winchester bottle was taken away for forensic examination, and a fresh set of fingerprints was found overlying the old ones made by previous legitimate handlers of the bottle. These fresh prints were clear impressions of the thumb and fingers of a man's left hand – it was much too large to be a woman's. The apparently naked footprints which had been noticed by the eagle-eyed nurse were found, on microscopic examination, to be the impressions of a man's stockinged feet, also of large size; minute fibres from red and blue woollen socks were found adhering to the polished floor. Similar fibres were also found on a window-ledge over which the intruder had climbed to gain admittance.

John Capstick asked every nurse in the hospital, as well as all porters, orderlies and other staff, if anyone or anything suspicious had been seen previous to the murder, and learned that on the previous night a prowler or Peeping Tom had been spotted shortly before midnight peering into windows in the nurses' residential block. He had been chased, but escaped. A nurse gave a good description of him and in four days he was traced, but his prints did not match those on the bottle, and he was able to prove that he was staying at his brother's house in a neighbouring town on the night in question.

As Chief Inspector Capstick was driven through the grounds to the child's body, which lay where it had been found, now covered with sheeting, he swore to himself a solemn oath that he would find her murderer, no matter how long it took and how great the cost in time and effort. In his own words, John Capstick has recorded his feelings as the Lancashire County Police photographer, Sergeant H.B. Taylor, took the requisite photographs of the body: 'I stared down at the pitiful form of June Anne Devaney, and I am not ashamed to say that I saw it through a mist of tears. Years of detective service had hardened me to many terrible things, but this tiny, pathetic body in its nightdress soaked with blood and mud was something no man could see unmoved. I swore, standing there in the rain, that I would bring her murderer to justice.'

Capstick lost no time in translating words into deeds. He was convinced that the killer was a local man, because only a native of the area would have known how to gain entry to, and exit from, the grounds of the hospital by way of an old quarry which lay adjoining the perimeter; there were clear and fresh signs of someone having broken through a chestnut paling fence at its weakest point opposite a gap in the hospital boundary wall, just by the quarry's edge. Chief Inspector Capstick was also able to say with certainty that the murderer was a very tall man, as only a man of well above average height would have been able to lift the child from her cot without dropping the side. Moreover, the footprints on the floor were ten and a half inches long – a man with feet of this size would most likely be above six feet in height, which subsequently proved to be the case.

The ridges of the fingerprints on the bottle were clear and unbroken, which pointed to the man being young, and not a manual worker. It was never known exactly why the bottle was left lying on the floor under the child's cot, but it would seem that as the killer entered the ward at a point near where the trolley of bottles stood, he decided to arm himself with one of them as a weapon of defence in the event of his being spotted and having to make a run for it; if a nurse had grabbed him by the arm, a blow from the heavy bottle would have enabled him to break free and make good his escape. Since the prints were of a left hand, the man was therefore probably left-handed.

Capstick was not a man to be easily discouraged. He decided upon an unprecedented course of action – to fingerprint the entire adult male population of Blackburn. This colossal task involved the taking of 50,000 sets of fingerprints and calling at no fewer than 35,000 houses, using squads of police-officers with inkpads and cards calling door-to-door. At the same time the officers were required to ascertain whether any male residents had been in Blackburn on the night of 14-15 May but had since left town. Various individuals were traced who had even left the country, some as far away as Singapore and America. This tremendous task took two months, plus an additional three weeks of work double-checking the issue of ration-books by the local Registration Office. This entire operation drew a complete blank.

Not to be daunted, Capstick then concentrated on released former inmates of mental hospitals and institutions. Over 4,000 men falling into this category were interviewed and fingerprinted. A further 3,000 sets of fingerprints were obtained from aliens residing in refugee camps in the area. The fingerprinting and interviewing was also extended to all known sex offenders who had been released from prison, and the tramps, vagrants and alcoholics who regularly – or irregularly – used the doss-houses and hostels in the district.

The Chief Inspector was planning his next move when he received a visit from Inspector William Barton, a Lancashire force officer who had been co-operating closely with the Yard's team. 'I've been checking and re-checking our files against the Electoral Roll,' he said, 'and I feel that somehow or other the man we want has slipped through the net. As far as we know, he's a young man – the prints on the Winchester bottle suggest as much. Could he be a serving soldier or airman? If so,' he pointed out, 'his name would not be shown on the Electoral Roll at all.' Wartime conditions had left their legacy of loopholes even in those post-war years ...

'What do you suggest we should do?' asked the Yard man.

Barton's local knowledge came to their aid. 'There is to be a new issue of ration-books due very shortly,' he told the Chief Inspector. 'I think we should check the ration-book file records against our fingerprint records. We may very well find that a few book-holders have been unaccounted for.'

Capstick was more than willing to try anything, after the taking of more than 50,000 sets of fingerprints had so far failed to turn up the wanted man.

A further 200 male persons, including many servicemen, were found by this means to have escaped the attentions of the officers who had carried out the check of the entire town. Their names and addresses were all registered at the local Food Office. Two constables named Lamb and Calvert were engaged in the task of sorting and correlating the fingerprints when the new batch of cards was brought to them containing the additional 200 sets of prints. A DI named Colin Campbell was responsible for checking each new set of prints against the photographed prints from the Winchester bottle.

As one of the cards, No. 46,253, from a house in Birley Street, Blackburn, was placed in position for the check by Campbell, he suddenly gave an excited shout.

Hospital of Horror

'I've got him! It's here!'

The other officers gathered round Campbell as he held the card aloft. They saw that the prints were those of a former guardsman named Peter Griffiths, twenty-two, of 31 Birley Street, Blackburn, now working as a packer in a flour mill.

There were some hasty consultations as to the best method of apprehending the suspect. As he worked the 10 p.m. night-shift, it was decided to wait for him in the street outside his home as he left to go to work that night. It was 12 August – almost three months after the most brutal and horrifying child murder John Capstick had ever experienced in his long career.

At nine o'clock that evening Capstick, accompanied by Inspector Barton and also Detective Sergeant Ernest Millen of the Yard's Murder Squad, who had been sent to join his team, was driven to the corner of Birley Street, a street of small terraced redbrick houses in a working-class area of the town. Leaving the car, they crossed the road and positioned themselves in the doorway of a house opposite No.31. After fifteen minutes the front door of No.31 opened and a very tall, slender young man walked out into the street, dressed in an open-necked shirt and dungarees, and started walking along Birley Street. John Capstick, the man who had sworn to catch the killer, grasped the arm of his quarry in a relentless grip, while Inspector Barton read him his rights after informing him that he was under arrest for the murder of June Anne Devaney at Queen's Park Hospital on the night of 14-15 May 1948.

'What's that got to do with me?' bluffed the suspect, giving each officer in turn a well-simulated blank stare. 'I've never been near the place.'

On the way to police headquarters in the car, the suspect repeated his denial, and was again cautioned, this time by Capstick himself. The suspect then lapsed into silence for some time before suddenly asking whether they wanted to interview him because of his fingerprints. The car drew up to the police-station and, as Griffiths stepped out, still held firmly in an officer's grasp, he suddenly stood still and turned to the policeman, saying,

'I suppose they're my fingerprints you found on the bottle. If so, I'll tell you all about it.'

Soon afterwards Peter Griffiths was making a formal statement, amounting to a confession of the crime. He began by describing his pub-crawl on the evening of 14 May, drinking thirteen pints of beer as well as a large quantity of rum. He then claimed that he had gone for a walk to clear his head when a stranger had offered him a lift in his car, dropping him near the hospital. This part of his statement was a lie, as no stranger had offered him a lift – he had deliberately hailed a taxi and told the driver to drop him at the quarry. At a subsequent identity parade the cab-driver had unhesitatingly picked out Griffiths as the man he had driven to the quarry, and in court at the trial he expressed the opinion that at the time he thought it very odd that a person would wish to be taken to that isolated spot at that time of night.

Continuing his statement, Griffiths claimed that the next thing he remembered was being outside a children's hospital ward. He left his shoes outside a door, which he tried and found unlocked. He opened it and went inside, where he could hear a nurse 'humming to herself and banging things as if she was washing up or something'. He picked up a bottle and walked half-way down the ward with it in his hand, then put it on the floor. His account of how he took the child from the ward is best described in his own words.

'I remember the child woke up and started to cry, and I hushed her. She then opened her eyes and saw me ... I picked her up out of the cot and took her outside by the same door. I carried her in my right arm, and she put her arms around my neck and I walked with her down the hospital field. I put her down on the grass.'

Continuing his statement, Griffiths made no mention of his frenzied sexual attack on the child, but admitted killing her, adding that he then returned to the veranda outside the ward, sat down and put his shoes on. He then went back to where he had left her, stating that he just stood looking at her without going up to her; then he went on straight across the field back to the quarry, and eventually reached his home some time around two o'clock. He stated that, after removing his collar and tie, he slept on the couch downstairs to avoid waking his parents by going upstairs to his own room.

After giving various details about his movements the following day, he ended his statement with the words: 'My mother and father asked me where I had been the previous night and what time I had come home. I said that I had been out boozing and had got home at twelve o'clock. This is all I can say. I'm sorry for both parents' sake and I hope I get what I deserve.'

After the statement had been signed and witnessed, Capstick had the unenviable task of returning to Griffiths's home to inform his parents. His mother, in tears, handed the Inspector a pawnticket which her son had left with her. It was for a suit which he had pawned for thirty shillings and eight pence. On its recovery from the pawnshop it was sent to the Forensic Science Laboratory at Preston, where it was found to be the suit Griffiths had worn at the time he committed the crime. Blood of Group A – the blood group of June Anne Devaney – was found on the trousers, and fibres found on the suit were identical to fibres from the dead child's nightdress. A pair of socks found at Griffiths's home was also found to be made of a material identical to the fibres found adhering to the polished floor of the ward and the window-ledge over which Griffiths had climbed.

A strange find at Griffiths's home was a sheet of notepaper among various letters and papers in his room, which bore the following verse. It was entitled 'Warning', and ran as follows:

> For lo and behold, when the beast
> Looked down upon the face of beauty
> It stayed its hand from killing
> And from that day on
> It was as one dead.

This verse was in Griffiths's handwriting, and was signed 'The Terror'. There was no date on the paper, and it is not known whether it had been written before or after the murder. It would seem more probable that the latter was the case, although this will never be known.

Griffiths's sorrowing parents stated to the police, and also later at the trial, that they had not noticed any change in their son's behaviour in the days following the murder, nor did he show any concern when his fingerprints were taken during the final check.

It was later discovered that Griffiths had been a patient at the hospital when he was a small boy, and that he had stayed in a ward in the same block as that in which C.3 was situated and was thus familiar with the layout of the children's wards.

Peter Griffiths was committed for trial at Lancaster Assizes and on Friday, 15 October 1948, he appeared in the dock before Mr Justice Oliver. His counsel put forward a plea of insanity, stating that he was a schizophrenic, but this did not impress the hard-headed Lancashire jury, who took less than twenty minutes to reach their unanimous verdict of guilty of murder. Griffiths remained completely unmoved as the judge sentenced him to death, and on Friday, 19 October 1948, he was hanged at Walton Prison.

8 Murder in the Blue Mountains

If it were not for the highway that cuts right through the little township of Lawson, New South Wales, it would be just a sleepy backwater. But the unending roar of traffic is a reminder that Lawson is a link in a chain of similar townships on the main route from Sydney to the farming and commercial growing centres of Western Australia. In Lawson, the Great Western Highway runs past the end of Henry Street where, at No.27, the Hart family – John and Emma and their three children – were living in 1969.

Six months earlier, the Blue Mountains township of Lawson had also been home to Ron Barton and his wife Yvonne and their five children, until Ron had been transferred by his firm to Locksley, about sixty miles away on the other side of the range towards Bathurst. The families had remained friends and kept in touch, and on the afternoon of Sunday, 12 January 1969, they were together again in Lawson. The Bartons' visit was intended to span several days.

On the following Wednesday, 15 January, Mrs Barton promised to take her youngest child, Victoria Ellen – known as Vicki – to nearby Wentworth Falls to visit one of the child's former school friends. That morning, the Bartons' other daughter, Kim, had an upset stomach. Ron Barton intended to catch the 1 p.m. train back to Locksley so as to be ready for work the next day, so Yvonne decided to take Kim to the local doctor's after seeing Ron off. She and the children intended to stay at the Harts' for a few days longer before returning home.

When Mrs Barton and Kim left the doctor's surgery they were surprised to find Ron outside. He had missed the train and would have to catch the 4.10 p.m. train instead.

After taking Kim back to the home of their friends, the couple had a few drinks in the Mountain View Hotel, then returned to the Harts' house in Henry Street. By now it was too late to take Vicki to visit her friend at Wentworth Falls, so to console her Yvonne agreed that she could accompany the other children to the swimming-pool in Lawson later in the afternoon.

At about 5.30 p.m. the children set out for the pool. Fourteen-year-old Anne Hart pushed her bicycle with ten-year-old Gary Barton riding on the machine. When the road became less steep, Anne mounted the bike, standing on the pedals, with Gary still sitting on the saddle, and they rode to the highway, about half a mile distant, along past the shops; Anne dropped Gary on the opposite side of the road, outside the railway station, while she went back for the other children. A subway runs under the railway station platform to Loftus Road on the opposite side, which is less than five minutes' walk to the swimming-pool. When Anne returned to the other children, Vicki was dawdling to the rear, so Anne picked her up bodily and sat her on the bike, then pedalled to the same shopping parade where she had gone previously. This time, however, she left Vicki outside the Mountain View Hotel, near the zebra crossing opposite the railway station, and told her to wait there while she rode back and shepherded the remaining four children. Several minutes later they all arrived at the place where Anne had left Vicki, but the child was nowhere to be seen. Anne naturally assumed that Vicki, against instructions, had crossed the highway and gone through the subway to the pool to join her brother Gary. Anne and the other children proceeded to the pool.

When they reached it at 6.15 p.m., there was no sign of Vicki, and Anne concluded that she had gone home instead, since her brother Gary said he had not seen her at all. At 7.30 the children returned home, and on learning that Vicki was not with them Mrs Barton borrowed Anne's bicycle and rode quickly to the pool to look for her, while Mrs Hart went to search the local park and playground, and Mrs Gallagher, a neighbour, went to look for her in a car-park behind the hotel where Anne had left her. By 8.15

p.m. Mrs Barton was frantic and called police headquarters in Wentworth Falls. No doubt she had more than a few words to say to Anne about leaving an eight-year-old unaccompanied in a busy street ...

Constable Starr, the duty officer at Wentworth Falls Police District Headquarters, alerted other officers in the area and initiated an all-night search for the child in Lawson and the surrounding district. The next morning an organized full-scale search went into operation, covering an area within a radius of nine miles in all directions from Lawson. The area was plotted in divisions on a grid and a police-officer placed in charge of police and civilian volunteers assigned to each division. They went over the scrub-covered slopes and gullies with a fine tooth comb while the Blue Mountains radio station, 2KA, broadcast bulletins throughout the day calling for any person with any information, however seemingly trivial, to come forward. No stone was to be left unturned for clues.

A life-sized clothing-store dummy was dressed in garments similar to those Vicki was wearing when she disappeared: a blue-and-white check shift-style dress with a rose pattern and red bias binding at the neck and armholes, black patent shoes, white bobby-socks and carrying a white cardigan. The disappearance was headlined in the *Sydney Morning Herald*, and scores of volunteers set out from Sydney to join in the search over the week end. Later the dummy model of Vicki was moved from outside the Mountain View Hotel, where Anne had left her, to a shop-window in a large store in Katoomba, the main town in the Blue Mountains area, to catch the attention of the Saturday shoppers. The dummy, complete with blonde wig, had a remarkable resemblance to the missing child.

It had been hoped that this dummy would jog the memories of persons who had been in the area at the material time, but no lead was forthcoming from this source. Almost 100 police-officers were now drafted to the search, and the civilian volunteers were augmented with dozens of civil defence workers, members of bushwalking clubs, church groups, servicemen on leave and working people on holiday. What the police found most puzzling was that literally no one seemed to remember having seen Vicki waiting outside the hotel in one of the busiest streets in Lawson in broad daylight. Two police-officers stood at the spot for two days, hoping they might spot some tiny clue – perhaps the odd behaviour of a person passing and repassing the spot for no valid reason. The general opinion that was held both by the police and the public was that Vicki had been abducted in a car; thousands of cars passed the spot every day. But if she had been dragged unwillingly into a car, surely someone must have noticed it? One school of thought believed she entered a car driven by someone she knew; even the New South Wales Police Commissioner subscribed to this view. After all, a child willingly getting into a car would not have drawn any attention to herself.

The police questioned all known child molesters, ex-mental patients and ex-prisoners with a history of crimes against children, but this drew a complete blank. All were able to account for their whereabouts at the material time. Ten days after Vicki had disappeared, the police reduced their search team; most people had by now given up any real hope that Vicki Barton would be found alive. Ron Barton returned to work after being given compassionate leave, and the family tried to settle down again to some semblance of normality. But it would never be the same again …

A year passed. On the first anniversary of Vicki's disappearance with the police no nearer a solution than they were at the beginning, a passing reference was made to the case in the Press when the Premier of New South Wales, Mr Askin, reminded the public that the five thousand dollars reward still stood. No one came forward to claim it.

On the afternoon of Saturday, 1 August 1970, at Springwood, fifteen miles from Lawson going towards Sydney, three children named Mark, Hanna and Rebecca Dostal were playing in the gully below their house. The gully, covered by bush and scrub, was an ideal place to play hide-and-seek. It was eight-year-old Hanna's turn to hide, and she scampered off into the surrounding undergrowth. As she ducked to avoid an overhanging branch, she caught a foot on something in the soil and stumbled. Looking down, she saw a human skull staring up at her, attached to a partly buried skeleton. Screaming hysterically, she rushed back to her brother and sister telling them she was going home. Her father tried to comfort her, telling her it was most likely the skeleton of a fox or some other animal which had died in the woods, but she refused to believe this, insisting that the skull was human – 'just like I've seen in books'. Mr Dostal decided to go and see for himself. What he found convinced him that his daughter had been right. It was the skull and skeleton of a small child, with strands of long blonde hair nearby.

A police car arrived shortly afterwards and constables searched the wooded section. Partly concealed by leaves, they found a child's black patent shoe and part of a white cardigan. Comparisons were made at the Sydney Dental Hospital between X-ray records of the jaw and the skull found at the burial site, but the police knew already that they had found the remains of Vicki Barton. Her parents were informed the following day; at last the waiting had ended ...

An all-out search for the murderer of Vicki Barton swung into operation, but with no leads to go on progress was impossible and eventually the operation was wound down, an inquest recording that the child had been murdered by a person or persons unknown.

In 1977, more than seven years after the finding of Vicki's remains, a man contacted Gerald Stone, the producer of a Channel 9 TV series on current affairs. The man was an ex-convict with a story to tell about people who were in prison for things they did not do while guilty men walked free. Pressed for further information, the ex-convict told Stone that he had known a man in Kirkconnel (a prison farm) who had told him that he had murdered Vicki Barton.

Stone drove to the Blue Mountains home of the man concerned and told him he had come to ask him some questions about the murder of Vicki Barton. The man refused to talk and called his mother, who told Stone to leave in no uncertain terms. Stone then contacted the police.

On 30 June 1977 a man named Alfred Jessop, aged twenty-four, appeared in court at Katoomba charged with the murder of Victoria Ellen Barton on 15 January 1969. Jessop was a nervous, thin man with a slight stammer, dressed in a green parka and jeans, who looked older than his years. A police witness said that he was married but separated from his wife and was living with his mother and brother, and that he was unemployed. Bail was refused.

Jessop was tried before Mr Justice Maxwell. His background spoke for itself. Police witnesses were able to show that the accused man had a long history of sex attacks on young girls, including his own sisters, and that when he was seventeen he had been admitted to a psychiatric hospital in an effort to cure him of his propensities. He had written to young schoolgirls through a Sunday newspaper pen-pal column and invited them to meet him outside the railway station in Lawson. In February 1972 he had been convicted of 'offensive behaviour' on railway premises, and on 26 June 1975 he had attacked a young woman near Parramatta railway station by throwing a rope round her neck like a lasso. For this offence he had been jailed for eighteen months.

The trial of Alfred Jessop lasted two days. He had admitted meeting Vicki Barton near the Mountain View Hotel (he was sixteen at the time) and persuading her to accompany him to a secluded area. He told police – according to the record – that he became annoyed with her when she refused to perform a sexual act with him, and he strangled her. He then placed the body in a small trailer attached to his bicycle and dumped it in the bush.

Alfred Jessop was found guilty and sentenced to life imprisonment, although he would be eligible for parole firstly because he was only sixteen at the time and secondly because the crime had been committed more than seven years previously. The judge commented on 'this useless and senseless killing of an innocent young girl' and pointed out that not only had a promising young life been destroyed but a family had been devastated beyond recovery, for it had broken up under the strain and the victim's parents were now divorced. Mrs Barton had also told a newspaper reporter that after years of being a practising and devout Catholic, she had now lost her faith in God completely.

Thus does the evil that men do live after them.

9 Two of a Kind

It is not often that two individuals will team up to go on what can only be described as a murder spree. But on 17 August 1967 Thomas Eugene Braun, a strapping six-foot eighteen-year-old of stocky build, and his best buddy Leonard Maine, also eighteen but slimmer and a couple of inches shorter, decided to do just that. Their orgy of death, maiming, rape, and joy-riding in stolen cars spanned three states.

On the day in question Tom (as he was known) left his job as a petrol pump attendant in a service depot at Ritzville, Washington, and went to pick up his friend Leonard Maine in his battered old black German-made Borgward open-top sedan. In the car were two guns, an automatic .22 Luger and a Frontier Colt single-action .22 pistol, plus several hundred rounds of ammunition.

'What, are you still driving that old boneshaker?' guffawed Leonard.

'Take your last look at it,' Tom said with a conspiratorial grin. 'We are going to have ourselves a new car.'

'How come?'

'You'll see,' was the enigmatic reply.

The two youths headed for Seattle, and on the evening of the first day of their impromptu mystery tour they stopped in the state capital and looked for a place to spend the night. When they inquired at a rooming-house in the city, the housekeeper at the establishment took one look at them and decided that they were up to no good. Let her now describe what ensued in her own words, as she was later to do: 'I suddenly saw a shadow in front of me as I spoke to them, and looking up I saw one of them was pointing a gun at me. I screamed and fled into an adjoining room and shut the door. I then heard a car zooming off noisily at speed, and presumed it was them.'

The record does not state where they spent that first night, but the following day they were heading along Route 202 outside Redmond, Washington, when they spotted an attractive 22-year-old girl driving a maroon Skylark. Looking at each other, the two smiled in secret agreement. Tom stepped on the gas. 'Watch this,' he told his friend.

Coming alongside the maroon car, which was being driven by Mrs Deanna Buse, married less than a year, who was returning from her job to her mother's house where she was staying at the time, Maine leaned out of the window and signalled frantically to the girl that something was wrong with a wheel, or wheels, of her car. Mrs Buse was, naturally, apprehensive; as she slowed her vehicle, the youths' car mounted the grass verge and pulled across in front of her, effectively cutting off her retreat. The young woman climbed out of her car, the youths meanwhile casting appreciative glances over her shapely figure. She walked around her car, examining each wheel in turn, but could find nothing amiss. As she stood upright again she gasped in horror as she saw that Tom Braun was pointing a gun at her head. He ordered her back into her car, and told Maine to return to their own car. 'You drive,' Braun said, 'while I hold the gun on this babe so she doesn't try any funny business.' Deanna decided that she had more chance of survival if she complied with the youth's orders. Maybe she might find an opportunity of escape later ...

The two cars drove slowly along the highway until they reached a turn-off, winding through a series of narrow side roads until they reached an unmade dirt road leading to a dead-end in woods near Echo Lake. Braun stopped the Skylark and pushed Mrs Buse in front of him, the gun's muzzle touching the back of her head; Maine alighted from the other car while Braun took Mrs Buse into the woods until they were lost from sight. A little later, as he stood beside the car, he heard five shots.

Shortly afterwards, Braun returned alone. He and Maine then drove both cars into Seattle and parked in a busy street near the city centre. They took their gear from their own car and transferred it to the Skylark, in which they then drove off.

Four days later a policeman, Sergeant Hart, was inspecting the abandoned Borgward, having been sent to do so by a patrolman owing to its having been left there unattended for four days. The police-officer's inspection turned up five .22 shell casings. He impounded the old car and reported in about it.

Just twenty-two miles south of Seattle, in Fife, Washington, Braun and Maine visited Maine's uncle, during the course of which they asked him what was the quickest route to Portland, Oregon. The next morning the pair crossed the state line into Oregon and, exhausted after their long drive, they tried to register at a motel; but the manager was very suspicious of the somewhat dishevelled-looking young fellows. He quizzed them about their car registration and asked for proof of identification, which they appeared to be reluctant to supply. Finally, the two backed out, returned to the highway and roared off in a cloud of dust.

Samuel Ledgerwood had just spent a most enjoyable day fishing. The lake was well stocked, and his catch had been impressive. Now, as the late afternoon gave place to a peaceful and quiet evening, Sam headed home in his late-model green Buick, well-pleased with his day's endeavours. He noticed two young men alongside the country road, trying to change a tyre. Being a friendly type of chap, Sam pulled over to help them, but it was to be the last Good Samaritan act he would ever perform. Indeed, he was so trusting by nature that he never noticed that the wheel the two youths had removed had absolutely nothing wrong with it; the tyre was intact and almost new.

Braun shot Ledgerwood through the head with two shots, the first of which killed him instantly. As he lay dead on the isolated logging road, the two youths set fire to Mrs Buse's Skylark car by firing several slugs into the petrol tank. They then piled their gear into Ledgerwood's gleaming new Buick and drove off.

The pair headed south, hugging the Pacific coast,

eventually arriving in northern California. Proceeding along the deserted mountainous Route 120, they encountered two young hitch-hikers, Susan Bartolomei, a young student, and her boyfriend, Timothy Luce, a student teacher from the same college. Both were seventeen. They were on holiday and had no particular destination in mind ...

At six o'clock the following morning, at a point along the same highway, a Mr and Mrs Mease, accompanied by their daughter and their nephew, were driving along in the direction of Santa Barbara when they saw a body lying in the road. They stopped their car to investigate. It was Susan Bartolomei. Mrs Mease felt the girl's pulse; she was still just barely alive. She gasped that 'they' had shot her and killed her boyfriend. She further elaborated that 'they' were two youths who appeared to be about eighteen years old, who said they were from Oklahoma and called each other 'Mike' and 'John'. An ambulance was sent for and Susan told her story to the police from a hospital bed. For several days she hung between life and death, but died about a week later from her injuries.

Back in Washington, searchers found the body of Deanna Buse in the wooded location where Braun had left her, stark-naked, with her clothes in a neat pile beside her. This feature gave police cause to believe that she had been forced to undress at gunpoint. She had been shot five times, including twice through the head. The pathologist, at the autopsy, could find no evidence of rape. Susan Bartolomei, however, had been raped several times before being shot.

In her few lucid moments between relapsing into a coma and regaining consciousness for brief periods, she furnished further details of the two young men's appearance and of their car, and asked the police to look for her boyfriend's body. It was later discovered that Braun had not only shot the boy dead but had also run over his chest with the car afterwards.

By now Oregon police had found Ledgerwood's body, and the manhunt was in full swing for the two suspects in the stolen green Buick as described by Susan Bartolomei. Police of three states were involved, and quite soon they

Two of a Kind

came up with some concrete clues – sooner, in fact, than they had anticipated. A few days later, in the hamlet of Jamestown, in California, a policeman named Ed Chaffee was making his early-morning patrol when he spotted a late-model green Buick with Oregon plates. It was parked in front of the little community's only small hotel. Chaffee was, of course, fully aware of the BOLO (be on the lookout for) call regarding a car of this description and also the two armed suspects. Chaffee looked over the Buick. 'When you've been in law enforcement as long as I have,' he was later quoted as saying, 'it often happens that you have a gut feeling about something. In this instance, I knew I was looking at the getaway car.'

Chaffee immediately radioed for back-up. He was not about to tackle two armed men alone; discretion was better than valour. Three officers answered the call and came to his assistance in less time than it takes to relate. Chaffee, in the meantime, had checked the hotel register, from which it appeared that 'Mike and John Ford', as they called themselves, posing as brothers, were in Rooms 19 and 26 respectively.

The three police-officers went upstairs to the rooms, guns drawn. Quietly they went to Room 19 with a passkey they had obtained from the manager. Slipping it noiselessly into the lock, the door opened only a few inches, being held by a safety chain. Through the gap they could see a young man, who was Leonard Maine, asleep in bed. One of the officers pointed his .38 through the opening and called out, 'Come out with your hands up and unlock the door chain.'

Leonard Maine, thus rudely awakened, climbed out of bed, clad only in a pair of underpants, and walked to the door. He unlocked the chain; when a pistol was pointed at *his* head, it was a different story and he was not one to argue. He was told to dress, and was then handcuffed to one of the officers, while the other two went to the next floor and kicked open the door of Room 26. The safety-chain lock broke loose from its moorings as they did so. Thomas Braun was in bed, his hand beneath the pillow as he made a grab for his gun. 'Watch out!' one of the officers shouted, and the other officer made a spectacular flying leap to the bed and jumped right on top of the suspect, who, while quick on the draw, was not quite quick enough. Pinning him beneath his weight, the officer quickly snapped on the handcuffs and retrieved the .22 from under the pillow. 'Get dressed!' was the terse order. The two policemen held him at gunpoint while the handcuffs were unlocked to allow him to slip his shirt and pullover over the vest he was wearing, and to pull on socks and trousers and lace his shoes. Then he was handcuffed once more. He asked to be allowed to change the boxer shorts he had been wearing for a pair of regular underpants, but he was refused.

Three months later, Braun and Maine sat impassively in court, their faces betraying no hint of their emotions. The prosecution produced one witness after another, with evidence so damning as to be irrefutable. Both movie and still photographs were shown of the victims Braun had killed; afterwards, both youths confessed to the murders.

Braun was sentenced to death while his accomplice was given life imprisonment. Both admitted all the details of their ghastly crimes – how they killed their unfortunate victims, when, and where; but one thing they never admitted to anyone was the reason why they had committed these crimes. Psychiatrists attempted to delve into the motives behind them, but the two young men remained obstinately silent.

Thomas Eugene Braun is still on death row in a Washington prison awaiting the execution of his sentence, and thus there may still be time for him to change his mind and agree to be interviewed by a psychiatrist and attempt to frame in words the reason, or reasons, behind the killing spree which he shared with his best friend. If he does, then the medical men who probe the disordered human mind may come up with not only an explanation but also, possibly, some practical pointers for the treatment of those similarly afflicted, and Braun will not die in vain.

10 Beauty in Distress

In the course of a series of psychiatric examinations conducted with a group of inmates in an American prison, one of the men, a convicted multiple murderer condemned to death and awaiting execution, was found to have an IQ of 130. The psychiatrists were amazed, because this man, Harvey Murray Glatman, was one of the most sadistic killers ever to step into San Quentin's gas chamber. It is, of course well known that criminals can have very high intelligence ratings, difficult as it sometimes is for the layman to believe it. The criminal mind is certainly not the monopoly of the dim-witted – far from it. A certain degree of intelligence is required to enable certain types of criminals to plan their crimes; after all, the better the planning the less liable they are to be caught.

Born in 1928 into a middle class family, Harvey Murray Glatman passed an uneventful childhood with no apparent problems, and was a model student at school – in fact he was voted 'the boy most likely to succeed' by the class of 1943. He had a 'thing' about ropes from an early age. An ardent Boy Scout, he carried off all the prizes for ropecraft and knot-tying competitions and passed an impressive array of badge tests involving proficiency with ropes, knots, signalling, pathfinding and so on. He is reported to have told a friend in his adult years, 'It seemed as if I always had a piece of rope in my hands, ever since I was a kid.'

His mother, however, was closer to him than his friends, the school or the Scouts and it was she who later stated that she had discovered, when he was about twelve years old, that he seemed to become what she described as 'a strange and secret child'. 'One evening,' she said, 'when my husband and I arrived home from a night out, we discovered that Harvey's neck was all red, with what looked like rope marks. He said that he had been up to the attic, taken a rope and tied it round his neck, which had made him feel good.' The Glatmans were mystified, and somewhat alarmed, by this manifestation of what seemed to be an incipient, precocious form of perversion, despite their son's tender years. They went to consult their family doctor, who gave them a supply of sedative tablets to give him, told them to ensure that he was kept fully occupied out of school hours, and finally assured them that he would 'grow out of it'.

By the time Harvey reached the age of seventeen, he was anxious to meet girls, but being very shy and introverted by nature, he could not face meeting them through the normal social channels. Instead, he invented a most unorthodox way of attracting their attention: he would snatch their purses in the street and run off. Then he would turn round and laugh, and throw their purses back to them or, on some occasions, hold the purse out for the girl to come and retrieve it. He could scarcely fail to meet girls by this method, but the girls themselves took a very dim view of it indeed.

Not surprisingly, Harvey's unique method of introduction proved completely unsuccessful, and not a single girl wanted to get to know him any better. One day, in desperation, on a main street in Boulder, Colorado, Harvey jumped in front of a young teenage girl, brandishing an imitation gun. Terrified, she screamed at the top of her voice, and he ran off. Police, armed with his description, soon apprehended him and booked him on a misdemeanour, but he was released on bond (a boyish prank, his counsel had called it). He skipped bond and fled to the East, where a few months later he was arrested in New York after committing a robbery. For this he got five years in Sing Sing.

He was still receiving psychiatric treatment at the time of his release from prison in 1951, and it seemed to all concerned that he had, apparently, reformed. He had been a model prisoner and caused no problems, and it was

Beauty in Distress

felt that he would make a good adjustment to the world outside. He moved to Los Angeles, where he opened a modest television repair business, and also took up photography as a hobby. 'Keep yourself fully occupied,' the prison doctor had recommended. Repairing television sets all day, and developing and printing films half the night, seemed as good a way as any of keeping oneself occupied. For six years Harvey Glatman led a quiet and uneventful bachelor life, never dating, and seldom speaking even to his customers beyond what was absolutely necessary. He gained a reputation for taciturnity, but that was not a crime.

The mild-mannered bachelor, however, was seething inwardly with frustration. He suffered increasingly from nightmares, and his inmost hidden thoughts – which he tried valiantly to hide even from himself – were thoughts of sex, perversion and death. It all came to a head on 1 August 1957, when his nightmares became a reality. On the afternoon of that day he met a pretty, recently married nineteen-year-old girl named Judy Ann Dull. When Harvey learned that Judy was a professional model, he told her that he was a freelance photographer 'on the side' from his television repair business, and that he had recently been commissioned by a New York-based detective magazine to photograph beautiful girls in distress – 'the typical bound-and-gagged stuff, you know, what they put on the covers'. There would be a fifty dollar payment for the girl if she were to agree to being photographed bound and gagged, putting on the most terrified expression she could on her face, while he operated a delayed shutter-timing device to enable him to be in the picture threatening her with a gun. 'It's only a toy gun,' he said. Judy agreed – fifty dollars was not a fee to be sneezed at.

Judy told him that she would first have to go home to change into some other clothes, and he offered to drive her there. As soon as she got into his car, he pulled a gun from his pocket. 'This is no toy, baby!' he said, caressing the gleaming barrel of his loaded .38. 'If you scream or try to escape, you've had it.' He then drove her to his apartment and frog-marched her up the stairs at gunpoint.

Once inside, he raped her several times, then bound and gagged her and placed her in an armchair, clad in black lace underwear which he produced from a drawerful of such items. He then photographed her, registering every detail of her terrified features as she strained against her bonds. Afterwards he raped her again, still gagged and bound, and then carried her, helpless, down the stairs to his car, and drove 125 miles into the desert east of Los Angeles. In a remote and isolated spot he threw her roughly out of the car, took more photographs of her, and then strangled her with what he was to refer to later as 'his favourite rope'. The last thing he did before leaving was to dig a shallow grave and place her body in it, still in its bonds.

Winds swept the sand from the grave and the girl's bleached skeleton was found five months later by a couple of hitch-hikers, but the lack of clues stymied the police. Glatman had enlarged photographs of his victim adorning the walls of his apartment, but of course these were only discovered much later.

Glatman now employed a different method to ensnare another victim. He joined a Lonely Hearts club in downtown Los Angeles, where he met Shirley Ann Bridgeford, aged thirty, a divorcee from Sun Valley, California. Glatman told Mrs Bridgeford that his name was George Williams and that he was a plumber. They made a date, and Glatman called for her at her apartment on 9 March 1958. Having told her that they would be dancing at an exclusive club, he asked her to wear formal dress. Mrs Bridgeford became somewhat apprehensive when Glatman headed the car towards the Anza-Borrego desert, a state park fifty-five miles east of San Diego. He explained that the club was, as he put it, 'out a ways'.

Once in the desert, Glatman now went through a now familiar procedure. He bound her hand and foot and gagged her, and used the same excuse about taking pictures for publication on the covers of detective magazines as an excuse to avoid alarming her. Once bound, Mrs Bridgeman was subjected to several rapes, after which he took the pictures, and then strangled her with the same rope he had used to kill his previous victim.

This time he did not bury his victim's body, but left it under a saguaro cactus.

On 23 July 1958 Glatman scanning the personal advertisements in a Los Angeles newspaper, noticed one which had been placed by Ruth Rita Mercado, a 24-year-old Puerto Rican model and part-time strip-tease artiste, who was seeking modelling assignments. Harvey rang the number given, and they arranged an appointment for him to go to her apartment. Once inside, he forced her to undress and raped her repeatedly. He then bound and gagged her and took her out into the desert, where he went through the usual routine of photographing her, purportedly for a magazine assignment. This time he took a good deal of time, and did not kill her until the early hours of the next morning. Here it is, perhaps, revealing to quote Glatman from his confession: 'It was not until much later that night that I decided to kill her. I did not really want to. She was the only one I really liked. I used the same rope in the same way.'

Glatman had now killed three pretty Los Angeles girls in the space of a year, yet the police had still no idea of the identity of the madman in their midst. If only they could have seen the pin-ups on the walls of Glatman's apartment! He had even had the temerity to include himself in pictures of the victims. And he was still free to carry on adding to the tally ...

His next choice was an attractive girl named Joanne Arena, aged twenty, but she proved to be too clever for the purveyor of beauties in distress. Having agreed to pose for some ordinary run-of-the-mill pin-up shots she insisted that she drive her own car and that she also bring a friend with her to the modelling session. Harvey told her to forget the whole thing, and thereby the girl undoubtedly saved her life. After Glatman's subsequent arrest, Joanne was quoted as saying, 'I'm not quite so dumb as I look. You know, I think he wanted to kill me. I knew it even then. I could feel it.'

Harvey's next victim was not quite so clever, but she was a fighter – someone who would not be killed without a fierce struggle for her life. Lorraine Vigil was a good-looking, statuesque 28-year-old brunette, who answered one of Glatman's advertisements in a Los Angeles paper for models. He told her that he would drive her to his studio. When they began to leave the city behind on the Santa Ana freeway, Lorraine became suspicious. Glatman swung the car on to the grass verge, produced a pistol, and tied her wrists. Later she was to tell police: 'I knew he was going to kill me. I tried to plead, but I knew that pleading wouldn't do any good. So I decided to fight.' She lunged towards him, and managed to grab his gun. A shot accidentally went off and wounded her in the thigh, but she continued to hold the gun on him. He tried to jump her to get the gun back, but they wrestled until both of them fell out of the car. He sprang to his feet, but the courageous girl held the gun trained on him from a sitting position.

Just at that moment a state patrolman, cruising along the freeway, saw them and pulled over. He came running, firing a shot into the air just as Glatman was about to spring on his fourth victim and wrest the gun from her. 'Freeze!' the patrolman yelled, his gun at the ready. Harvey Glatman froze.

In custody, later that same day, Glatman bragged, 'If I'd wanted to I could have killed that highway patrolman who arrested me.' He then recounted each of his rapes and murders, giving every detail. The police praised the courage of the girl who had brought about his capture at the risk of her life. Glatman's potential fourth victim had undoubtedly saved the lives of many others who would have fallen into his clutches if he had gone free.

Three days afterwards he was convicted of murder, and expressed a willingness to die. While he was on death row in San Quentin, his lawyers tried to arrange appeals on his behalf, but he refused to co-operate, saying he preferred to die. He told them: 'It's better this way. I knew this was the way it would be.'

On 18 August 1959 he had his wish. He forfeited his life in the gas chamber in San Quentin – not that it could have brought back the girls whose lives he snuffed out and whose bodies he left in the California desert to become sun-bleached skeletons. His last words, whatever they might have been, are unrecorded. Since he was able to prove that for six years he could live as a law-abiding citizen without giving way to his homicidal impulses, one is led to wonder what it was that triggered his murderous rampage.

11   The Melbourne Strangler

The afternoon of Saturday, 9 November 1930, was warm and sunny – it is of course spring at this time in Australia. School was out, and Faulkner Park, in Melbourne's inner suburb of South Yarra, was full of children happily playing the traditional games – hopscotch, hide-and-seek, tag, and other favourites. The swings and roundabouts, too, were busy and the park resounded with the carefree voices of youth.

One small group of little girls was romping noisily in the sun while, unseen by them, a man dressed in workman's overalls stood in the shadows watching, his face bronzed and impassive beneath his wide-brimmed felt hat. As one of the girls ran past him he called out to her and she stopped in her tracks. He asked her if she would like to take a message for him to a friend who he said was waiting for him outside the park gates. The twelve-year-old, Mena Griffiths, hesitated for only a moment or two, then nodded. Together they walked across the park towards the road, and as they did so one of Mena's younger sisters, eight-year-old Joyce, rushed up to her to ask her where she was off to. 'Just going on a message,' she explained, adding that she would be right back.

Mena accompanied the thin-faced, sharp-featured man in the felt hat and work-stained overalls along busy Punt Road, which was in the opposite direction to her house in Caroline Street, chatting pleasantly to the somewhat taciturn stranger, who had won her confidence with his slow smile. They walked for about a mile and a half to the bayside suburb of St Kilda, where the man bought bags of fish and chips for them both. She told the man at this point that her sisters in the park would be wondering why she was taking so long and, anyway, where was the person she was to deliver the message to, and what *was* the message?

The man pointed to a house (which was standing empty) in Wheatley Road, Ormond, an adjoining suburb, as they approached it. Boy, this was a lot of walking just for a message, she told him. They went up the overgrown path to the front door. 'They never lock the door,' he said as he pushed it open ...

One is led to wonder why a girl as old as Mena Griffiths would not have queried why she was needed to deliver the message. Surely the man could have delivered it himself? And in any case Ormond was a great distance from the park gates.

When Mena Griffiths did not return to her sisters in the park they went home and told their parents that she had gone off with the stranger, apparently to deliver a message, and had said that she would not be long. They also gave a fairly good description of the man, except that they thought he was 'about fifty' – he was in fact thirty-five. Little children (Mena's sisters were eight and six) tend to overestimate people's ages – anyone over about twenty or so is 'old' to them! However, when their parents gave the man's description to the police, the latter knew that they would have a difficult task – after all, hundreds, perhaps thousands, of workmen in Melbourne wore overalls and felt hats, and had tanned faces from their outdoor labouring jobs.

It was two small boys, eight-year-old John Carstairs and his ten-year-old brother David, who found Mena's body the next morning as they played in the derelict house in Wheatley Road. She was lying face down on a pile of rubble. Her hands had been tied behind her back with strips torn from her own underclothing, and her ankles had been tied together with the same material. A gag made from her white bobbysocks had been thrust into her mouth. Thumb prints on her neck indicated strangulation as the cause of death. The autopsy showed no signs of sexual assault. The police, however, knew that some sex perverts are incapable of the act of rape and obtain sexual satisfaction during the course of other acts such as strangling or choking their victims. They checked on all known perverts south of the Yarra River.

Nine weeks later, with the police no nearer a solution to the killing, sixteen-year-old Hazel Wilson walked out of her house in Melton Avenue, Ormond. It was a Friday evening and she was bound for a dance-hall with a school-friend, wearing a new floral-patterned dress and her first high-heeled shoes. It was almost, but not quite, dark when she left home.

When she did not return home her disappearance was reported to the police, but once again it was not the police who found her. It was her brother Frank who, having spent the whole time since dawn the following day looking for her, found her body shortly after midday, lying in some bushes on a vacant lot in Oakleigh Road, Ormond. The blue belt of her dress had been used to tie her hands behind her back, and her ankles had been tied together with strips torn from her panties. A stocking had been pushed into her mouth as a gag and held in place with more strips from the panties. She had been strangled, but not raped. The place was less than a mile from the house where Mena Griffiths had been found.

One curious fact revealed by the autopsies on both victims was that the tying of the limbs had been carried out *after* the strangulation. The two killings were indisputably the work of the same man: the second was a carbon copy of the first, except that the second victim was a teenager and not a girl just burgeoning into puberty.

Police did not find any connection between the two dead girls, who had not known each other. Police were forced to conclude that they had been killed by a ritual murderer who probably achieved orgasm only by strangling and tying up a dead body. Known deviates from all over Melbourne and district were rounded up and brought in to headquarters for questioning, but every one had a water-tight alibi. Finally, police inquiries reached a dead-end. The names of Mena Griffiths and Hazel Wilson faded from the newspapers; only their families and friends mourned.

Four years elapsed, and there were no more ritual strangulation-and-bondage murders of young girls. The police heaved a sigh of relief. Children were allowed out to play unsupervised. Young girls walked after dark to reach dance-halls, youth clubs and evening classes, or to meet their friends in the coffee bars. Very few of the general public in Melbourne even remembered the names of Mena Griffiths and Hazel Wilson.

New Year's Day, 1935, dawned bright and sunny. It was the height of the Australian summer and people were making the best of it. A number of families met for a bumper picnic at Inverloch, a beach resort near Melbourne. Late that same afternoon twelve-year-old Ethel Belshaw from nearby Darwin Meadows, dressed in a white frock and with her long fair hair in plaits tied with white ribbons, went into a shop, accompanied by her friend eight-year-old Margaret Knight, to buy an ice-cream. Ethel was served first and went outside the shop to wait for her friend, and stood licking her ice-cream while Margaret was being served. When Margaret came out, Ethel had vanished. It had happened in less time than it takes to tell.

The next day Ethel's body was found in a scrubby area not far from the shop by a man walking his dog. The body was strangled and tied in exactly the same fashion as the two victims of four years before. The Melbourne police were soon under heavy fire from Press and government. Police questioned thousands of people who had been in the busy area at the time the girl disappeared, but no one had seen a thing. An eighteen-year-old youth, the brother of Margaret Knight, was arrested, but was soon set free after it was proved that he was elsewhere at the time. In his nervousness he had given conflicting answers when questioned by the police. In any case four years' previously he would have been barely fourteen.

One of the thousands of men questioned routinely by the police during the investigation was a man named Arnold Sodeman, who had a criminal record, although the police were unaware of this at the time. In 1918, when he was eighteen, he received twelve months for forgery. Soon after his release he and another man held up and wounded the station-master at Surrey Hills railway station a few miles east of Melbourne. Sodeman was sentenced to three years' hard labour. While he was being transferred from Pentridge prison to another prison he escaped, but he was quickly caught and a further year was added to his sentence. Following his release in May 1926 he appeared to go straight. He married, and the couple had a daughter.

During the Depression he travelled from place to place with his wife and child to wherever he could find labouring jobs, mostly in rural areas. At one time he was living in Ormond. His usual employment was as a navvy in a roadworking gang.

Police inquiries continued all through 1935, Inspector Superintendent J. O'Keefe keeping heavy pressure on all his men. On the night of Sunday 1 December 1935, a child was reported missing to the police at Leongatha, sixty-seven miles from Melbourne. June Rushmer, aged six, had left a recreation ground that evening at dusk to walk home, but she never arrived. Her body was found the next morning in McPherson Lane, about half a mile from her home. Her death by strangulation and binding after death were an exact replica of the three earlier crimes, and a huge contingent of detectives rushed to Leongatha from Melbourne in record time.

This time the murderer had almost certainly been seen. Two boys reported seeing a man in a dark suit riding a bicycle without lights, but neither of the boys could identify or describe him. It could have been anybody. So this promising lead petered out, much to the chagrin of the police.

As is so often the case, it was the murderer himself who tripped himself up. Arnold Sodeman was at that time living in Leongatha and was working with a road construction gang at Dumbalk, thirteen miles away. A few days after the finding of June Rushmer's body, the men were sitting yarning around a camp-fire during a tea-break when the subject switched to the murder of the little girl. One of the men said to Arnold, who was sitting quietly smoking his pipe, 'Didn't I see you out there that day riding your bike?'

The effect on Arnold was electric. 'No, you bloody well didn't!' he shouted, rising to his feet and flinging the remains of his tea into the fire as he strode off to his quarters.

The man who had made the remark in the first place pondered on Arnold's reaction for some time before deciding to report it to the police. It was so unusual for the man to blow his top like that, he explained. Usually he was the quietest man on the site and rarely ruffled by anything or anybody. It was too suspicious, he thought, to let the incident pass unnoticed.

A squad car full of detectives raced to the site from their temporary mobile incident headquarters at Leongatha and brought Arnold in for questioning. Under expert interrogation, Arnold broke down and confessed. He told the detectives that he had left home to cycle back to the camp on Sunday night after the weekend break. As he pedalled along, he saw little June, whom he knew, tripping along the footpath. She called out to him, and he stopped and lifted her in his arms and sat her on the crossbar of his bike. After cycling a short distance, he dismounted and put her down, telling her she could walk home the rest of the way as it was not far. As she skipped off, he dropped his bike at the side of the road and ran after her. She looked back at him, and something in his manner frightened her and she ran off to hide in the bush. 'I ran after her and caught her around the neck,' Arnold told police, 'and when she began to scream I stuffed a gag into her mouth.' He then described how he had strangled her until she went limp and then bound her with strips of her underclothing, and tied her belt across her mouth to hold the gag in place.

He also gave police full details of the three previous murders, all the time speaking in a soft, matter-of-fact voice entirely devoid of emotion. He made no mention of any sexual feeling accompanying his acts, but this does not of course exclude the possibility – even probability – that he achieved orgasm at some point. Men of this type – shy, inarticulate – frequently find it embarrassing to try to describe their sexual feelings, and may actually find it easier to describe murders they commit.

As the news of his arrest and confession permeated the little community, his neighbours and others who knew him spread their hands in disbelief. All who knew Arnold Sodeman and his wife and their eight-year-old daughter

Joan said that they had always considered them to be an exemplary family. As Arnold languished in the Leongatha lock-up, men boozing in the hotels were saying 'The bastard ought to be lynched!' and started making plans how to spirit him out of the cell and carry out their intentions. The police soon realised that they had a serious problem on their hands, and just in time they managed to get him out of the rear entrance in the dead of night and rush him in an unmarked car at high speed to Melbourne and put him in prison under heavy guard.

Arnold Sodeman was charged only with the murder of June Rushmer, his trial opening at the Melbourne Criminal Court on 17 February 1936. The defence entered a plea of insanity, but the court refused to accept it. Several doctors stated that the accused man was not conscious of what he was doing when under the influence of alcohol, but it was pointed out that he had given a lucid account of the murders to the police and in court he gave brief, intelligent answers to all questions which were put to him. He appeared in court neatly dressed in a grey sports suit and a yellow shirt open at the neck, which set off his ruddy complexion and made him appear younger than his thirty-five years. He appeared at ease in court, and in his cell was quiet and well-behaved, quite composed and evincing little interest in his case. The jury, unimpressed by the defence of insanity, found him guilty, and he was sentenced to death. His counsel appealed, but this was refused by the Appeal Court of Victoria, and the legal process was instituted which led to an application to the High Court of Australia, asking for a retrial on various legal grounds.

The four senior judges of the High Court were equally divided in their opinion, which led to the appeal being dismissed. Despite the horrific nature of the crimes, however, many people believed that Sodeman was insane at the time of the murders and therefore could not be held responsible for his actions. These people believed that the execution of the prisoner would be a grave miscarriage of justice, and because of the growing support for his case the Government of Victoria consented to the case going before the Privy Council in London. On 28 May a despatch was received from the Privy Council's Judiciary Committee rejecting the application, and on 2 June Arnold Sodeman went to his account by the hand of the hangman in Pentridge Jail.

'I am ashamed of what I have done,' Sodeman had written in a letter to a senior detective. 'But at the time, I just have a dull kind of feeling that I must do what I am doing. After a few glasses of beer, I lose control.'

An autopsy was carried out on his body, and this showed that 'the gentle family man' suffered from leptomeningitis, a chronic inflammation of the meninges (a part of the brain). This flared up under the influence of alcohol and caused him to lose control of his actions – a true case of insanity while under the influence of drink. Today a man could live with this condition without causing anyone any harm provided that he had treatment for alcoholism and undertook not to drink liquor in any form. But in those days these things were little understood, and the miscarriage of justice which put to death a mentally sick man was permitted to take place. Moreover, it did no one else any good, for it would not bring back the murdered children to their grieving families.

12 A Forensic Triumph

Already famous for thirty years, the forensic pathologist Richard Kockel, in his laboratory at the Institute of Forensic Medicine at the University of Leipzig, in what is now East Germany, was the obvious choice whenever a tricky question came up concerning a corpse in a difficult homicide investigation. So the Nordstern Insurance Company, one of the largest in the area, had no second thoughts about making an appointment to send one of their agents to see Dr Kockel.

At about noon one day in late November 1929 the agent arrived on his urgent and confidential mission. There was a body in the funeral chapel of the Leipzig Southern Cemetery which was due to be buried in less than an hour. The dead man was one Erich Tetzner, a Leipzig businessman born in 1903, who had been the victim of a car crash. According to the police report, he had been driving his green Opel along Highway 8 on 27 November 1929 when it collided with a milestone, caught fire and Tetzner, trapped in the driver's seat, had been burnt to death. The authorities had released the body for burial.

The problem, as far as the insurance company was concerned, was that Tetzner was found to have taken out accident insurance not only with Nordstern but also with two other insurance companies. Moreover, the total of the sums insured amounted to 145,000 marks – an enormous sum in those days for a man of his financial status. These insurance policies had come into force only a few weeks prior to the accident. Tetzner's widow Emma (née Georgi) had applied for payment of all three policies immediately after her husband's death. Such circumstances inevitably aroused a certain amount of suspicion on the part of the insurers. Of course, it was quite possible that Tetzner had suffered from a heart condition which he had not disclosed to the companies concerned in his proposal form, or indeed might not even have known about, and would have died at the wheel of his car; on the other hand, there was the possibility of suicide. In any case, after much persuasion, the widow had eventually consented to an autopsy. There was no time to have the body removed to the Institute; would Kockel be willing to perform the autopsy at the chapel?

The doctor agreed, postponed his lunch, and drove out to the cemetery with the insurance agent.

In the coffin lay what he later described as 'a badly-charred trunk to which were still attached the cervical segment of the vertebral column together with the base of the skull, the upper halves of both thighs, the lower articular extremity of the right femur, and parts of the arms. In addition, along with the corpse was a portion of brain about the size of a man's fist.'

It was soon determined that the body was that of a slightly-built man. The male organs were charred, but still recognizable. No trace of hair could be found on the head, since the top of the skull was missing. The portion of brain was in remarkably fresh condition; Kockel found this difficult to account for. In the mouth, the larynx and what was left of the windpipe, he found sooty deposits. The heart contained a little viscous blood. The lower lobe of the right lung was well-preserved. Kockel transferred the blood from the heart and the lobe of the lung into vials and put them into his bag.

He then examined the bones of the corpse, and was startled to find that they were unusually frail. His astonishment increased when, on sawing through the well-preserved articular head of the humerus, he immediately recognised the remains of a cartilage which extends between the articular extremities of the long bones only in the young. In the course of human growth these cartilages disappear by the age of about twenty. Kockel asked the agent once again how old the victim had been. 'Twenty-six,' was the reply. 'How tall was Herr Tetzner?' asked Kockel. The agent looked through his

A Forensic Triumph

documents. 'He was five feet eight, broad-shouldered, stocky build, somewhat obese,' he replied.

The muted voices of the funeral guests could be heard in the ante-room as Kockel left the chapel by a rear exit. As he walked towards his car there leapt to his mind a case which had given a great deal of trouble to the police, a professor of forensic medicine in another city, and two insurance companies the previous year.

On 1 January 1928 a 32-year-old Fulda businessman named Heinrich Alberdin had said good-bye to his wife and set out for Frankfurt, ostensibly to go to the theatre. Since then he had not been heard of. Early in February the Fulda police received a letter which had been posted in Regensburg a few days earlier. It had been written by Heinrich Alberdin, stating that he was throwing the letter out of a window and asking the finder to post it. He was being held captive by two business rivals, he stated, since he had stumbled upon their trade in narcotics. They had drugged and kidnapped him on the way to Frankfurt. If he were found dead, the police should look in the lining in the right sleeve of his jacket.

Seven months later, on 23 August 1928, a male skeleton was found in a thicket near Saalfeld. He had been shot through the head, the feet amputated and the clothing scorched. On the bone of the right-hand ring finger a wedding-ring engraved 'M.T.1920' was found, and in the waistcoat pocket a watch engraved 'H.Alberdin, Fulda'. In the lining of the right-hand sleeve of the jacket a signed letter in Alberdin's handwriting was found, containing such sentences as 'I must now prepare myself for my last journey, I am told. If anything should happen to me inform the police in Fulda at once. My name and address are Heinrich Alberdin, 24 Marktstrasse, Fulda.'

As soon as Alberdin's widow had been informed of her husband's death, she presented her claims to two life insurance companies for a total of 60,000 marks. The two policies had been taken out in September 1927 – less than five months before Alberdin's disappearance. In the meantime Professor Giese of Jena had been asked to examine the remains. From the stage of development of the spinal column he determined that the body could not possibly be the body of a man of thirty-two but at most that of a young man of twenty to twenty-two. At the same time Professor Stadtmüller, The Göttingen anatomist, demonstrated by another method that the dead man could not be Alberdin by superimposing drawings of the skull of the corpse, drawn on transparent paper, upon photographs of Alberdin's head enlarged to life-size. Striking differences on the shape of the skull and of the head immediately became apparent. Alberdin had vanished, and it seemed extremely likely that a stranger had been killed in order to deceive the insurance companies. Briefly, the outcome of the case was that in 1934 the police, acting on a tip-off, made a sudden raid on Alberdin's house, where they found him hiding under the bed. He was sentenced to death for murder; the victim was never identified.

Kockel, remembering this case, turned to the insurance agent as they were leaving the cemetery, and asked him whether he was certain that the dead man was Erich Tetzner. 'Do you doubt it?' asked the agent. 'I certainly do,' Kockel replied, 'but I will reserve my final answer until later this afternoon.'

At that time forensic medicine could look back upon nearly a hundred years of research into various types of burns, and death by burning. One of the most important discoveries was that people who had been exposed to fire while alive inhaled soot, which could be detected in the windpipe and in the lungs. It was also found that carbon monoxide, which is produced in all forms of combustion, is also inhaled and is therefore present in the blood of those who are burnt to death.

With the increased number of accidental and suicidal deaths occurring after the introduction of gas for domestic lighting around the middle of the nineteenth century, forensic experts learned to look for evidence of carbon monoxide in the blood of such victims. There is a strong affinity between carbon monoxide and haemoglobin, the colouring matter of the red blood corpuscles. This affinity is stronger than that between the haemoglobin and the oxygen which is vital to life. Carbon monoxide kills by displacing the oxygen in the haemoglobin.

The red colouring of carboxyhaemoglobin is more resistant to discoloration than the pigment of oxyhaemoglobin, and forensic experts availed themselves of this principle to detect carbon monoxide in the blood. If blood is exposed to certain chemicals, normal oxyhaemoglobin quickly assumes a brownish colour, while carboxyhaemoglobin remains red. Spectroscopic analysis of blood proved even more efficient than chemical tests. When exposed to certain reagents, the spectral lines of oxyhaemoglobin change, while those of carboxyhaemoglobin do not. However, there must be at least 20% carbon monoxide present for this test to work.

In 1928 Schwarzacher, in Austria, perfected a number of methods which produced results with a significantly smaller percentage of carbon monoxide in the blood. Kockel was, of course, well-conversant with all these developments, and by three o'clock in the afternoon of 30 November 1929 he was back at the Institute examining the blood specimens he had taken for the presence of carbon monoxide. He applied all chemical and spectroscopic tests, and the results were uniformly negative. This reinforced his original feeling that the body was not that of Erich Tetzner, for if there was no soot in the respiratory passages and no carbon monoxide in the blood, the victim could not have been alive and breathing when the car burst into flames. Was there a possible parallel here to the Alberdin case? Had Tetzner, the ostensible victim, murdered a stranger and burned the body in his car so that his wife could collect the insurance?

The next step was to determine whether the victim had been subjected to violence *before* the fire. This involved another branch of forensic pathology. Some years previously, medical scientists had observed that one of the effects of violence was to drive fat from the tissues into the blood-vessels. This happened after fractures caused by skull beatings, sometimes even after light concussion. Particles of fat travelled with the bloodstream into the right chamber of the heart, and from there into the lungs. The consequence might be blockage of the small blood-vessels of the lungs, thus producing rapid death by stopping the circulation. If the circulation was vigorous enough it drove particles of fat to other parts of the body, including the kidneys and the brain. Sometimes these fatty embolisms could develop within the space of a few seconds. They were always the result of some kind of external trauma. When they were found in the lungs, this always betokened a grave injury received *before* the body was burned, and on this basis Kockel concluded that the victim in the cemetery chapel had in all probability been murdered before being burned.

By this time evening had fallen. Nevertheless Kockel, who in the course of his work had established a close relationship with the police, decided to inform the Leipzig police at once. Herr Kriegern, the police chief, was sceptical at first, but Kockel laid before him a plausible theory, its main points being as follows: (1) The dead man was not Erich Tetzner. (2) The corpse was that of some unknown man who had first been killed and his body then burned. (3) The killer was probably Tetzner, who was attempting an insurance fraud. (4) The missing body parts – the top of the skull, the lower legs – could not possibly have been consumed in the fire. Parts of the head had probably been removed because they showed fatal injuries; the lower limbs had probably been amputated because they would have revealed that the body was not that of Tetzner at all. It would be essential to search the whole area in the vicinity of the car crash for these missing parts. (5) Tetzner was doubtless in hiding and would try to get in touch with his wife.

That same night Police Chief Kriegern gave orders for Erich Tetzner's home to be watched, and the next day it was learned that Frau Tetzner was using a neighbour's telephone with unaccustomed frequency. He promptly had this line tapped. At the same time he sent a search squad to the scene of the accident; however, nothing was found. It did, however, turn up the information that Police Inspector Pfeiffer, who had been the first to arrive at the scene of the wreck, had discovered the uncharred portion of brain which Kockel had examined during his autopsy *outside* the burnt-out car, about five feet away, on the side opposite the driver's seat. Chief Kriegern passed this significant fact on to Kockel, who took occasion to point

A Forensic Triumph

out once more that a forensic specialist should have been called out to the scene immediately.

Shortly afterwards, Kriegern received an interesting report from the Ingoldstadt police. A locksmith named Alois Ortner had been in the local hospital since 22 November. He stated that on 21 November the driver of a green Opel had offered him a ride. Just outside Ingoldstadt the driver had said that something was wrong with the car and asked Ortner to crawl under it and tighten some bolts. When Ortner emerged from under the car he received two violent blows to the head and shoulders. Stumbling to his feet, he saw that his attacker was the hitherto friendly driver, who was now wielding a wrench raised ready to strike him again. Injured though he was, Ortner grappled with him, and finally broke free and fled into the woods. Since Tetzner's car had been a green Opel, he might have been the mysterious attacker. Had he chosen Ortner at random for his victim, the enterprise failing because Ortner proved too strong for him?

At 8 a.m. on 4 December the detective tapping Frau Tetzner's telephone line had a long-distance call from Strasbourg. The caller gave an Italian name, Stanelli. The detective switched into the line and said that Frau Tetzner could not be reached and would not be home until six o'clock that evening, when Herr Stanelli should call again. The detective noted that the caller's voice did not sound like an Italian – more like a German. Meanwhile the call had been traced to a booth in Strasbourg's main post-office.

Kriegern contacted the Sûreté and asked to have French detectives watch the post-office. He took a special plane to Strasbourg – an unusual course of action in those days – arriving just in time to arrest the man who entered the booth a few minutes before six o'clock. His surprise was so great that 'Stanelli' admitted that he was in fact Erich Tetzner.

That night he made a full confession. In September, he admitted, he had developed his plan for an insurance fraud. After taking out three insurance policies, he had set out to look for a suitable victim. He admitted that on 21 November he had lured Alois Ortner into his car and had tried to kill him. Before setting out on 26 November to seek a new victim, he gave his wife detailed instructions. If he carried out his coup, he would send her a telegram describing the victim's clothing. She was to give these particulars to the police *before* she was shown the body to identify it. In a short while she was to put in the insurance claims. He would then ring her at intervals giving a false name to the operator, and after the insurance money was collected he would arrange to meet her abroad.

On 27 November he had seen a hitch-hiker on the highway going to Regensburg. The hiker's appearance did not resemble his own; he was of frail build and considerably younger than himself, but after his experience with Ortner he preferred a victim who was his physical inferior. On his way to Regensburg the hiker fell asleep. Tetzner cautiously headed his car into a milestone, when his passenger awoke briefly. Tetzner explained to him that he had had only a minor accident. As soon as the young man had drifted off to sleep again Tetzner poured petrol over the car from a reserve tank he had, and tossed a burning match on to the car. When the car went up in flames he ran off.

Kriegern discussed the case at length with Kockel, who said that he considered the confession to be false. What about the fatty embolism in the lungs? The stranger had not been killed by the fire, Kockel insisted, but by prior violence. Moreover, the police findings supported the medical deductions; for example, how could the dead man have been found in the driver's seat if he had fallen asleep in the passenger seat and supposedly have been burnt to death there?

Kriegern interrogated Tetzner several times, but each time he stuck to his story, until in April 1930 Kockel's complete written affidavit was shown to him. Then, suddenly, he repudiated his first confession. Kriegern had given him enough time to familiarize himself with the contents of the affidavit, and apparently Tetzner, after some reflection, had realized that the presence of fatty embolism was in fact a point of indubitable proof of prior violence. He saw in this a chance to escape the full penalty for his crime. Early in May he asked to see the examining magistrates.

A Forensic Triumph

He admitted that his previous confession was false. In the dark of night, his story now ran, he knocked over a hiker. Finding the man unconscious in the road, he lifted him into his car. A few moments later he realized that the man was dead, and the idea suddenly occurred to him to use this stranger as a victim for his insurance fraud plan. He therefore placed the body behind the steering-wheel and set fire to the car. This new confession was undoubtedly clever; it supplied an explanation for the fatty embolism, and at the same time cleared him of the imputation of having first murdered his victim. A car crash and an insurance swindle were, after all, less serious charges than murder ...

On 17 March 1931 the trial of Erich Tetzner and his wife Emma began in Regensburg. Kockel produced his autopsy findings in support of the prosecution's claim that Tetzner had murdered the unknown stranger – who, like Alberdin's victim in 1928, was never identified – before setting fire to his car. Kockel proceeded to show how essential it was to link the theory of forensic medicine to the realities of any given cases. If Tetzner's victim had been burnt alive in the car, he asked, how could the portion of unburned brain, which indisputably came from the dead man, come to be lying on the road five feet from the burnt-out car, on the driver's side? How else could one explain it than by the same conclusion to which the presence of a fatty embolism had led him – that Tetzner had killed his victim outside the car and cut off those parts of the body that would have betrayed his act, obviously losing or overlooking the portion of brain in the process? The defendant, Kockel maintained, first killed and mutilated his victim, and then burned the dead man's body in his car.

Tetzner was convicted and sentenced to death. On 2 June 1931 his appeal for mercy was denied, and he was executed at Regensburg on 2 May 1931. His wife was given a life sentence as an accessory to the fraud plot.

Thanks to Kockel, forensic medicine was by that time devoting more attention to the problem of fatty embolism, and developing procedures for determining whether a burned body had been alive or dead at the time of the burning. It was discovered that carbon monoxide could enter the blood even of persons already dead through the skin. The presence of carbon monoxide in the blood-vessels close to the skin was therefore no proof that it had been inhaled during a fire. Only if the gas were found in the blood of the heart could it be assumed that the victim had been burned alive.

It was found that soot could penetrate deep into the bronchiae of cadavers, but never into the very finest branches, known as the alveoli. If soot were found in these, it had been inhaled during life.

Forensic research also discovered which types of injuries inflicted on a burned body with criminal intent could still be discerned after burning. For example, the marks of strangulation withstood the action of fire, whereas breaks in the larynx, such as a fractured hyoid, which for so long had been considered clear evidence of choking or hanging, could be produced solely by the heat of flames, without preceding strangulation.

In this way Kockel was able to discount yet a third confession which Erich Tetzner made after his appeal for clemency failed. He said that he had taken the hitch-hiker with him all the way from Reichenbach, and that shortly before they reached Nuremberg the man complained that he felt cold. Tetzner stopped the car and swaddled him in a car rug so tightly that he was helpless, and then strangled him before setting the blaze. Even this third and final version fell far short of the truth. No signs of strangulation had been discerned on the corpse; forensic pathology had triumphed again.

Three years later, on 19 January 1934, Richard Kockel died from cancer of the trachea, and his name passed into legend.

13 'If at First you Don't Succeed ...'

When a wife is found murdered the husband is usually the first suspect. Accordingly the Gardaí, within fifteen minutes of seeing the bloody corpse of thirty-nine-year-old Ellen Fleming on the floor of her kitchen on 26 July 1933, set off for the house where her husband was known to be spending the evening. Little more than half an hour later Detective Sergeant Byrne, after the usual preliminaries, was telling John Fleming that he was arresting him on a charge of murder, whereupon Fleming replied, 'I will go with you,' *without asking who had been murdered*! An innocent man would, at the very least, have inquired who was the victim; even a guilty man would most likely do so as a precaution. But no innocent man would agree to be arrested for a murder he knew nothing about!

The dead woman had married John Fleming in 1931. Two years later they were living in Drumcondra, a Dublin suburb. Fleming, who was thirty-four, worked as a shoe salesman in a Dublin store; his wife worked in another shop in the city.

At about midnight on 31 March 1932 Mrs Fleming was taken violently ill. Fleming sent his wife's young nephew, who was staying with them at the time, to summon a next-door neighbour, Mrs O'Rourke, saying that his aunt had 'had a stroke'. Mrs O'Rourke came immediately, ran upstairs to the bedroom and found Mrs Fleming in bed, in obvious agony. She was in the grip of a severe spasm, with staring eyes, opening and clenching her hands and gritting her teeth. Though barely able to speak, she managed to ask Mrs O'Rourke to rub her arms and legs. Mrs O'Rourke did her best to help, and in a few minutes her brother-in-law, Patrick O'Rourke, arrived.

O'Rourke was a qualified dispensing chemist and knew, just by looking at the sick woman, whose spasms were now becoming more severe, that this was certainly no stroke. When her lower jaw dropped he knew this for a bad sign, if his suspicions were correct. He called John Fleming, who was downstairs, and advised him to fetch the doctor – advice one would have thought unnecessary to a husband whose wife was in such obvious distress. Fleming came into the room with a glass of hot milk which he offered to his wife. She refused it, with the question, 'Why do you insist on my taking it, John?' He did not press the matter, but left the room, taking the milk with him, and the O'Rourkes assumed him to be going to fetch the doctor.

In a few minutes, however, he was back again, this time with a wineglass containing some coloured liquid which, he told his wife in answer to her question, was 'a mixture of port and whiskey'. She was now able to speak more easily. 'It is not!' she said. 'We don't have any in the house.'

'There was just a little in the very bottom of the bottles,' replied Fleming, offering her the glass. She tasted it and spat it out immediately. 'It tastes just like those chocolates you gave me the other day – bitter!' she complained, putting the glass down on the bedside table, whereupon Fleming took it and left the room, saying that he was going for the doctor.

It was now about 1.45 a.m. and Mrs Fleming was still seriously distressed. Her husband went downstairs to the kitchen, and Patrick O'Rourke, becoming suspicious, followed him into the kitchen, where he found him holding the glass under the running cold tap; the coloured liquid had disappeared.

O'Rourke spoke plainly. 'If anything happens to Nellie (Mrs Fleming) I will hold you responsible,' he said. 'I can find a doctor in the wilds of Connemara in half an hour, so it's jolly queer that you can't get one in the city of Dublin in an hour and a half.' To this Fleming replied, 'I will get a doctor,' and went out; but he returned without having contacted Dr Cotter, who had been his wife's physician for years, or Dr Shiel who lived only a few minutes' walk from the house. Fleming then went out a second time and returned still without Dr Cotter, saying that the doctor's maid had told him from her bedroom window that the doctor was out. This was a lie; he had not even knocked at the doctor's door.

Fleming then went out a third time, again supposedly to bring a doctor, but again returned alone. Finally the O'Rourkes insisted that at least a nurse should be called, and sent the young nephew to fetch a Nurse McDonagh who lived nearby. She arrived at 2.45 a.m.

When the nurse asked Fleming what was wrong with his wife, he replied, 'She has just had a bad turn, that's all' – an astonishing statement in view of the fact that she had presented an alarming appearance for over two hours. Patrick O'Rourke, from his experience, felt certain that it was a case of strychnine poisoning, although he did not voice his suspicions. Even the nurse was taken aback when Fleming added gratuitously, 'She is getting on a bit, you know.' After all, Mrs Fleming was not yet forty!

Nurse McDonagh applied hot fomentations to Mrs Fleming's legs and to her lower jaw to ease the stiffness and spasms. Mrs Fleming then slept, and Nurse McDonagh stayed with her. Fleming came into the bedroom one or twice to inquire 'whether he could do anything', but not once did he ask the nurse what was wrong with his wife. At 8.30 a.m. he left for work.

At midday Nurse McDonagh sent for Dr Cotter, and when Fleming came home from work for lunch the doctor was there. 'I have seen your wife,' he told Fleming. 'She is suffering from nerves, and she needs a tonic.' From this it was clear that Dr Cotter had not been informed of the symptoms that she had displayed the previous night, which were the classical symptoms of strychnine poisoning ...

Fleming's reply to the doctor was either brilliant or exceptionally stupid, depending on one's point of view. 'Yes,' he said, 'I know it was only nerves she was suffering from. I only pretended to go for you last night.'

Early the next morning, before going off to work, Fleming had called in at the O'Rourkes'. 'About those chocolates,' he volunteered. 'I was in the country recently and asked Joe (Mrs Fleming's brother) to get me some strychnine from the chemist to poison the dog next door. It might have worked loose in my pocket and got into the chocolates. I buried the rest of it in the back lane. For the life o'ye don't be telling Nellie, or Maggie O'Brien' (a neighbour and friend of his wife).

The two listened in silence to this remarkable recital, as well they might, for Fleming was now for all intents and purposes admitting that he knew his wife had not had a stroke but had been poisoned, and that despite her grave symptoms he had not procured a doctor or even sent for the nurse (Fleming's treatment of his wife that night was called 'disgraceful' by prosecuting counsel at his subsequent trial – an understatement indeed). Mrs O'Rourke said nothing, but her husband commented, 'It is dangerous to carry stuff like that around in your pocket.' 'If Nellie had eaten the chocolates would she have died in an hour?' persisted Fleming. O'Rourke was taken back, but answered, 'It might take three hours.'

O'Rourke's suspicions that Mrs Fleming's symptoms had been those of strychnine poisoning were verified by medical evidence at the trial. O'Rourke was asked by the defence whether he had not thought it his duty to report his suspicions to the Gardaí if he had suspected that Fleming was trying to poison his wife. His answer was that once nursing and medical aid had been provided the responsibility was no longer his.

A few days later Mrs Fleming left her home and went to stay with her sister on the English mainland for a few months. One might surmise that she was afraid of what her husband might do to her, for there had been trouble between them once before. She had reproached him for not going to Mass during Easter, and he had lost his temper and assaulted her, causing quite severe injuries.

On Wednesday, 26 July 1933, the weekly half-day for both the Flemings, Mrs Fleming, now back again in Drumcondra, came home from work at 1.30 p.m. Her husband came home shortly afterwards, and both were seen in the tiny back garden of the house. Fleming was weeding a flower-bed and Mrs Fleming was chatting with Mrs O'Rourke over the garden wall: 'After I've tidied the

'If at First you Don't Succeed ...'

house I'm going to meet my sister off the seven o'clock train.' Fleming was nearby and could hear every word his wife said. The sister referred to was not the one she had stayed with in England but another sister who lived about ten miles from Dublin and whose son was the boy who often stayed with the Flemings.

After some further small-talk the women separated, but met again later, and the last time Mrs O'Rourke saw Mrs Fleming alive was at about 4.30 p.m. at her own door, still wearing the working overall she had worn earlier. Fleming was then in the back garden cutting the grass with a pair of shears, and Mrs O'Rourke was about to leave for the city to meet a woman friend.

At 5 p.m. Mrs Fleming, still wearing her overall, crossed the road to speak to a neighbour, and left her ten minutes later to return home. That was the last time she was seen alive.

At 6.30 Mrs O'Rourke returned from the city and saw that the back door of the Fleming house was closed and that nobody was about, and that the windows, which had been open, were also closed. Fleming was last seen at the house at about 4.30. He was next seen at about 7.30 or 7.35 when he arrived at the house of his friends the Ryans in Clontarf, where he was later arrested. He appeared perfectly normal as he came in through the back entrance and greeted the maid who was working in the kitchen. 'I've just been to Dollymount' (a beach about three miles from Drumcondra), he said. 'I've had a good swim, and I did some sunbathing.' Going through the kitchen into the dining-room, he met his hostess. 'I've been to Dollymount – I'm sorry I'm late,' he said, and then repeated what he had said to the maid about his swimming and sunbathing. It was observed that he had no towel or bathing costume with him nor was his hair damp.

Meanwhile, Mrs Fleming's sister and nephew arrived in Dublin by train at 7.20, and as Mrs Fleming was not at the station to meet them they took a cab to the house, arriving fifteen minutes later. There was no reply to their knock, so they went next-door to borrow the key from the O'Rourkes. The boy left his mother with them while he let himself into the house. When he reached the kitchen door at the end of the hall he found that he could open it only a few inches, as there was something on the floor which prevented him from opening it further. He managed to squeeze his head through the opening, and he gasped in horror when he discovered that the obstruction was his aunt's blood-soaked dead body.

He immediately ran for help. Garda Wilson and Dr Shiel were the first on the scene and forced the door sufficiently to enable them to get into the kitchen, where the doctor was able to make a preliminary examination of the body. Mrs Fleming was no longer wearing her overall but was dressed as though to go out, wearing a hat, jumper and skirt, all of which were saturated with blood, and a large pool of blood had formed under her. Her upper denture was lying on the floor, and her spectacles were partly on her face. A necklace, its clasp broken, lay upon her chest. The one window in the room was secured by a bolt on the inside, and the room was in an orderly and undisturbed condition. Mrs Fleming's unopened handbag lay on the table and contained about four pounds, so clearly robbery had not been the motive for the murder.

Leading off from the kitchen was a scullery, the door from which led into the back garden. This door was unbolted, as was the gate from the garden to the so-called 'back lane' which ran the length of the road and parallel with it. Clearly the assailant could have left by this route. There were no bloodstains in the bathroom, which adjoined the scullery nor in any of the waste-pipes, and there was no evidence that the bath, the wash-basin or the sink had been recently used. Fleming owned four hammers which he kept in a tool-shed, also used as a coal shed, in the garden; one of these was missing. It had a blunt, rounded edge on one side and a sharp edge on the other.

According to Dr Shiel, Mrs Fleming had been dead between two and three hours, but could have been dead for only one and a half hours, although he thought not. His opinion was based on the body temperature which, however, he estimated by touch and not with a thermometer, as he did not have one with him. As Mrs Fleming had been seen alive at 5.10 p.m. and had been found dead at 7.40 p.m., Dr Shiel's estimate of three hours was incorrect; two and a half hours was the maximum. So she had died not later than at about 5.40 p.m.

The dead woman's injuries were horrendous. She had been struck twenty times, which suggested a frenzied attack. The first blow probably felled her; it, and some of the subsequent blows, had been administered with a blunt instrument, while others had been dealt with a fist. There were several separate skull fractures, lacerations over the right eye and ear, and heavy bruising on her forearms, indicating that she had put up a tremendous struggle to defend herself. There was no sign of any sexual assault.

Back in Clontarf at the Ryans' house, John Fleming was working in the garden with his friends' young son. He said that he had cut his right index finger with his garden shears at home, and asked Mrs Ryan to help him bandage it, as the cut was bleeding profusely. At the time he was wearing blue trousers and waistcoat and a brown striped shirt; the jacket to this suit was hanging on a hook in the hall. Later in the evening the cut finger started to bleed again. Fleming washed it, but did not re-bandage it. He called attention to this second bleeding, and the next day at work pointed out the cut to two fellow-workers. When he came in after work to the Ryans' house he was asked whether his finger had stopped bleeding, and he said that it had bled again that morning at work.

When Detective Sergeant Byrne and two other Gardaí arrived at 9 p.m., two of them pushed Fleming roughly to one side, and when Mr Ryan came forward to find out what all the commotion was about one of the Gardaí intercepted him and told him, out of Fleming's hearing, that Mrs Fleming had been found dead. Fleming was wearing the same blue suit that he had worn the night before, but this time with a white shirt. Byrne drew attention to some spots at the front and on the left sleeve and cuff, remarking that they looked like blood, but made no mention of murder. Fleming told Byrne that he had cut his finger the evening before while working in his garden, and showed him the cut.

After arresting him, Byrne asked Fleming for his shirt, collar and tie, which he handed over, borrowing replacements from Mr Ryan. He was then taken to the Garda station where his suit, shoes and socks were removed and replaced with others brought from his home. To all that had happened Fleming had responded with docility, and never once asked, nor was he told, who had been murdered, until 1.20 a.m., when he was charged with the murder of his wife. He made a brief statement: 'I know nothing about it, because I was not at home at that time. It was between 4.30 and 4.45 p.m. when I left home ... My wife was waiting for Mr Cunningham, the insurance agent, who lives at 7 Dargle Road, to call.' That was all he said, and at no time did he show any concern that his wife had been murdered nor ask how it had happened; he seemed totally indifferent.

Fleming's trial lasted from 14 to 21 November 1933. Fleming was defended by Mr Sean Hooper, then a young junior counsel, whose able performance in the case brought him to the forefront of the Irish Bar. For the prosecution were Mr Martin Maguire and Mr Kevin Haugh. The judge was Mr Justice Creed-Meredith, KC, a Chancery lawyer with little or no criminal experience.

As Mr Maguire was opening the case he was about to mention the poisoning incidents of March 1932 and the incident of Fleming's assault on his wife when Mr Hooper objected. The jury was sent out while the legal points were argued. Mr Hooper urged that the prosecution could not cite these matters in evidence because to do so would violate the fundamental rule that evidence of an offence other than the one being tried may not be given. But an exception to this rule is where relations between accused and victim are demonstrated by other evidence tending to show a pattern of behaviour, such other evidence being connected with a previous attempt by the accused upon the life of the victim; it is then open to the prosecution to adduce 'evidence of system' to corroborate a previous attempt, or attempts, at murder. The judge held that in the present case this exception applied, and that the attempted murder by poisoning could be put into evidence, but ruled that the physical assault could not.

The other evidence that the prosecution would produce, to show what kind of feelings Fleming harboured towards his wife, was that, apparently unknown to her, he had been conducting an affair with a young girl for about four years. He was twenty-nine when he had met this girl, Rita Murtagh, then only sixteen, who was a waitress in a Dublin restaurant where he lunched daily. After about a year Fleming invited her out and a friendship began, but intimacy did not take place between them until the third year of their association. Fleming deceived this girl, who had become deeply attached to him, by telling her that he was unmarried and lived with his aunt, and promising to marry her. As long as his wife lived he could never honour his promise, for in Catholic Ireland there was no divorce. The girl believed and trusted him implicitly, visiting his house when his 'aunt' was away.

If Fleming had wished to keep his affair with Rita Murtagh secret he had gone the wrong way about it. His house was in a narrow road of small lower middle-class houses close together in two long terraces, in which privacy was at a premium. Neighbours must have seen the girl go in and out, and were of course perfectly well aware that Mrs Fleming was absent from home on these occasions. The houses had no front gardens, the doors opening directly on to the footpath, and so built that the front doors were in pairs almost touching each other. It would be difficult for anyone to go in or out of any house without the knowledge of the occupants of the second house in each pair. Fleming had also taken Rita Murtagh to a local hall and sat with her in full view of many of his neighbours, which provided the gossips with plenty of material for their wagging tongues. Yet, curiously enough, Mrs Fleming seemed to have been unaware of these rumours, though it would seem unlikely that some of the many women who knew her did not drop her a hint or two.

Gossip, too, had reached the girl's family in July 1933. Her mother was called to give evidence of a talk she had had with Fleming in that month about the rumour which had reached her husband and herself that Fleming was a married man. At this time he had announced his engagement to Rita, and when her parents asked him bluntly whether he was indeed free to marry he replied,

'As far as I am concerned, I can marry your daughter next month.' At this time, unknown to her parents, she was pregnant, and as the baby was due in September she would not be able to conceal the fact much longer. Rita's father recounted in the witness-box that Fleming had assured him that he was single and lived with his aunt, and said that the rumour about his being a married man was due to women's jealousy. 'My aunt keeps house for me,' he said, 'and I sometimes take her out for walks.'

The next witness was a jeweller who told of Fleming and the girl coming into his shop in February to choose an engagement-ring and a wedding-ring. Fleming did not pay for them at the time but asked to have them put aside for him until he could come back in a few days' time. He never did come back, nor pay for the rings, and after a week the jeweller put them back into his stock.

Rita Murtagh now gave evidence, punctuated by sobbing as Fleming's perfidy was exposed to the glaring light of day. When, in January 1933 she told him of her condition, he appeared overjoyed. 'It was always my ambition to have children,' he said. This was probably true, for there had been only one child of his marriage and that had been stillborn, and it was very unlikely that his wife would again conceive, doctors had said. His apparent delight gave no hint to the girl of her predicament. 'Of course we'll be married soon?' she asked. 'Yes, before Lent,' was the reply.

Some weeks after the visit to the jeweller, the rings not having materialized, the girl asked Fleming when she would receive them, for she had naturally told her parents and friends that the rings had been chosen. He gave the excuse that he was 'getting some money from the bank, but first he had to obtain a signature for it, and this was the cause of the delay'. She never did receive the rings, but he frequently reassured her about their forthcoming marriage, and in March 1933 he told her that it would take place 'as soon as his aunt left the house to return to the country in a few months' time'.

By this time Rita was becoming uneasy, as the date for her confinement daily drew nearer but that for her wedding did not. On 20 July, sick with anxiety and fearful that her parents would discover her secret, she told him that there was a rumour going around that he was already married. Fleming laughed at this and called it absurd, saying it was old wives' tittle-tattle because they had nothing better to do. But she was not satisfied. 'You must prove to my parents that you are not married,' she demanded. Fleming still would not admit the truth, and concocted another lie. 'There are two Flemings in my street and the other one is married,' he explained. 'They must have got us confused.'

After placating her father with these falsehoods, Fleming met Rita briefly on 24 July – two days before the murder – and arranged to meet that evening, but he failed to turn up. He also failed to keep another appointment which had been made for 26 July. The girl never saw Fleming again after 24 July until the trial. Her child was born on 22 September.

During Mr Maguire's questioning Rita Murtagh had borne herself with reasonable composure and had told her story coherently, but when Mr Hooper started to cross-examine her she showed obvious distress, broke down, and then fainted and had to be carried from the court. A doctor examined her and said that she was unfit to continue further that day with her evidence. This was, of course, most difficult for Mr Hooper, and might have been disastrous for his client, but fortunately there was no real point of controversy in her remaining evidence and the only matter Mr Hooper wanted to establish was that the suggestion of marriage had come from the girl and not from Fleming. She was able to resume giving evidence the next day, by which time she was sufficiently composed to answer questions on this point, her replies substantially agreeing with what was adroitly being suggested to her. She was then allowed to leave the court and go home.

Mr McGrath, the State forensic pathologist, now gave evidence of finding nine small human blood spots or splashes on Fleming's waistcoat, seven on one trouser leg below the knee, and thirty on the left sleeve of his jacket between the elbow and the wrist. His white shirt bore four spots about four inches below the neck, seven on the left cuff and one on the left sleeve just below the shoulder.

These, too, seemed to be splash spots. He said that some of them could, possibly, be attributed to bleeding from a badly-cut finger, but in this case he would have expected to find blood on other parts of the garments. He considered it unlikely that blood could have found its way on to the jacket sleeve merely by taking cigarettes out of the pocket with the injured hand. Some attempt, he continued, had been made to wipe off or otherwise remove the spots or stains on the trouser-leg, and although a jacket button had been wiped there was still a small residue of blood on the thread which held it to the jacket.

On cross-examination Mr Hooper made the point that since there were no traces of blood in the sink, wash-basin or bath waste-pipes Fleming could not have been the murderer. Of major importance, he emphasized, was the question: *whose* blood had fallen on Fleming's clothing? The pathologist could not say, since he had not been furnished with a specimen of either Fleming's or his wife's blood – a most curious omission.

The insurance collector Cunningham now testified that he had called upon Mrs Fleming at 4 p.m. to collect some insurance premiums and his superior, a Mr McPartland who had been working with him that day, was produced as a witness to corroborate him as to the time. But a woman who had been living opposite said that she had seen the agent call at 4.50 p.m., and if she was right then Fleming could have been telling the truth in saying that his wife was waiting for Cunningham when he left. Either way, the exact time of the agent's call could not be clarified with any degree of certainty, so the real question still remained: when *did* Fleming leave the house?

In a sense, Mr Hooper was right in that the only evidence was circumstantial: a few spots of blood, a missing hammer, and the accused's failure to ask the Detective Sergeant who had been murdered. Yet it was highly improbable that anyone else could have murdered Mrs Fleming. Could anyone visualize a stranger in broad daylight entering the house stealthily by some means or another, risking being seen by several neighbours, murdering Mrs Fleming undetected, without stealing anything or attempting a sexual assault? At dead of night, yes, maybe; but not on a bright July afternoon, in a house which stood cheek by jowl with several others. It was inconceivable.

Fleming now took the oath and commenced his own evidence. He freely admitted his association with Rita Murtagh, that she had become pregnant, and that he was the father of her child. He admitted that when she told him of her condition in January 1933 and asked him to marry her he had agreed, and they had visited the jeweller and chosen two rings.

The poisoning incidents took some explaining. Fleming stuck to his story that he wanted the poison to kill the dog next door, and emphatically denied ever having attempted to poison his wife in any way, repeating the unlikely story he had told the O'Rourkes about the poison getting into the chocolates in his pocket. He accounted for the blood on his clothing from the copious bleeding of his badly-cut finger.

Asked how he had spent the afternoon of the day of the murder, he said that after arriving home at about 1.30 p.m. and lunching with his wife, they had discussed some new houses being built on another road in Drumcondra. His wife wanted him to look at them as they had been thinking of moving. After speaking to the O'Rourkes he went upstairs and took four pounds in cash from a tin kept in the wardrobe. On the way down again he met his wife coming up and asked her whether she was ready to come out with him. She said not, as she had to wait in for Mr Cunningham. So, Fleming said, he went out without her, leaving at about 4.30 by the front door – it might have been 4.45. No one saw him go out, and the prosecution contended that he had left by the back door to avoid being seen.

Fleming then described in detail how he spent the time from that point until he reached Clontarf. He had looked at the new houses, as his wife had requested, and had then taken a bus to the beach, swam and sunbathed without a costume, leaving his clothes on the beach, dried himself in the sun, dressed, and then continued into Clontarf. In the whole of those three hours he had met no person he knew, and so could not support his alibi.

The judge spotted several weak points in this narrative. It

seemed likely, he said, that Fleming had invented this house-hunting excuse, not considering its implications. Why should he not have waited for his wife, or have been asked by her to wait until she was ready to come with him, for such an important matter which concerned them both? It was their half-day, and they would not have another free afternoon for a week. Then, again, when he arrived at the Ryans' he made no mention of having looked at any houses: a small point, perhaps, but very significant in view of the fact that Mr Ryan was his best friend and said during his evidence that he had no idea at any time that the couple contemplated moving.

Fleming's supposed wish to poison the dog also looked very thin when subjected to cross-examination. For one thing, he had never been known to complain about the dog to its owner, with whom he was on cordial neighbourly terms, and the reason he had sworn to for wanting to kill the dog was that 'the dog's house was separated from his kitchen by only a thin wall, and the odours from the dog pervaded his kitchen.' This, on the face of it, seemed patently absurd. There was a normal brick-and-plaster wall between Fleming's kitchen and the next-door garden where the dog's kennel was situated. Fleming had also said that he had put the poison into some sandwiches which he had laid in the next-door garden after dark. No one had seen the remains of any sandwiches in the garden, nor had the dog shown any ill effects.

As Fleming returned to the dock, his counsel stood to make his final speech to the jury. It was an unenviable task, but Mr Hooper made two good points. He asked how a man who wanted to poison his wife would be so stupid as to ask her own brother for the poison. Indeed, the very question makes it seem absurdly improbable that Fleming could have intended murder, until one remembers his failure to fetch a doctor and his lies about trying to do so – not to mention his three attempts to induce his wife to consume the poison ... Dr Cotter, when called as a witness, had made it quite clear that there had been no call from Fleming, or on his behalf, for his services on the night in question and if there had been he would have responded immediately.

Mr Hooper's second point stressed a fundamental legal principle, namely, that a jury could convict a person of murder only if they were satisfied beyond any reasonable doubt that the person was guilty. But it was clear that the jury were, in effect, also trying Fleming for the attempted murder by poison, and Hooper urged that Fleming was entitled to have this attempt proved or otherwise beyond any reasonable doubt, and said that as they were not satisfied about this attempt then there must be a doubt about it. They should, therefore, before proceeding further with their deliberations, find the poisoning attempt not proven. Only then, their minds freed from the overwhelming prejudice of the poisoning incidents, could they hope to give Fleming what was his legal right – a fair trial on the murder charge. 'For all you know,' continued Mr Hooper, 'it was mere misadventure that the poison got on to the chocolates, and that Fleming, when he realized this, decided to take advantage of it by not fetching a doctor. If that is what happened, and his wife had died in consequence of his neglect that night, it would have been manslaughter and not murder.'

The judge's charge to the jury supported Mr Hooper on these two points, but otherwise was unfavourable to Fleming. He pointed out that, when considering whether Fleming had told the truth in court, they were entitled to bear in mind all the lies he had told the girl and her parents. 'Can you, then,' he said, 'place much reliance upon his statements now as to the route he took, and just accept them because he said so and there is difficulty in proving or disproving them? ... Some people tell lies with great facility, and the strange thing is that they expect to be believed. If they are queried they reply, "I have said so; can you disprove it?" ' This was as good as telling the jury that Fleming was an habitual liar, whereas the fact was that he had made many unfavourable admissions against himself, corroborating several prosecution witnesses. An habitual liar would have denied anything which could tell against him.

The judge implicitly supported the prosecution's theory that the murderer must have left the house by the back door, maintaining that he could not have opened the kitchen door, enabling him to leave the other way, owing to the obstruction of Mrs Fleming's body, which was proved by the pathologist not to have been moved after it had fallen. The prosecution had also pointed out that the murderer must have known that she would be at home that afternoon, she had not been sexually assaulted, nor had there been any robbery. Taking all these facts into consideration, they could scarcely entertain any further doubt as to Fleming's guilt.

The jury then retired to consider their verdict, and in two hours they brought back a unanimous verdict of guilty. When the judge asked Fleming whether he had anything to say as to why sentence of death should not be passed upon him, he replied, 'I am not guilty, my lord. I wish to make an appeal.' He remained calm and composed as he stood to attention in the dock.

After the sentencing, Mr Hooper asked for leave to appeal, which the judge granted on the legal ground as to whether the evidence regarding the poisoning should have been admitted, but it availed Fleming nothing. The Court of Criminal Appeal, holding that this evidence had been properly admitted, dismissed the application.

John Fleming was executed in Dublin on 5 January 1934.

14 The Desert Killer

Charles Howard Schmid was the only son of well-to-do parents in Tucson, Arizona, who ran a nursing home for the elderly set in acres of grounds just outside the city. The young Charles, despite his short stature, became an athletic champion in high school. He liked to wear cowboy boots stuffed with newspaper to make him look taller, and used to brag about imaginary heroic exploits in an effort to win a spurious kind of popularity from the more naïve of his teenage friends. Occasionally he was asked why he had an odd shambling gait (caused by the stuffed boots) and would say that he had been crippled in a fight with Mafia hoods. But few believed him.

His wealthy parents believed that if they indulged his every whim they would keep him out of trouble. One of the things they did was to allow him the exclusive use of his own bungalow in the grounds. Charles would spend most of his time driving around in his car visiting the student haunts of the university town and picking up young co-eds (American college girls), whom he would try to impress with his tall stories, and more often than not he would bring them back to his bungalow and seduce them. One girl, Mary French, fell in love with him, and Charles told her that the best way she could prove it would be for her to work for him. He obtained a job for her in his parents' nursing home and forced her to pay her wages into his bank account.

At twenty-two, Charles seemed to exercise a peculiar fascination for teenagers, both girls and boys. As a result, girls flocked round him, which enabled him to lead a highly-involved sex life, even if this was not as hyperactive as he liked to boast. He claimed that he knew a hundred different ways of making love. He also gathered around him a coterie of young men who called themselves his buddies and regarded him as a macho figure to be imitated.

In May 1964 he began to feel that mere seduction was becoming repetitive and boring. One evening, in the company of Mary French and one of his friends named John Saunders, Charles jumped up suddenly, shouting, 'I am going to kill a girl tonight, just to see what it feels like.' His girlfriend and buddy ignored his outburst, attributing it to over-indulgence in alcohol, or perhaps drugs. They all decided to go out for a drive in the car, and visited the home of a fifteen-year-old girl named Alleen Rowe, whose mother was, they knew, out at work as a nurse on the night-shift at the local hospital. Mary French persuaded Alleen to come out for a drive with them.

Out in the desert, near a deserted golf-links, Charles dragged Alleen from the car and raped her, and then killed her with a rock. The other two, who were sitting in the car, could hear the girl's screams, which suddenly stopped. 'My God,' Saunders said, 'Charlie has gone mad. He must be hyped up to the eyeballs on dope. I never imagined he would actually do it. I thought we were just going out for a boozing picnic.' Mary French was too shocked and horrified to say very much, but she bitterly regretted having invited Alleen to go with them.

Charles came back to the car. 'I've buried her,' he said. He then kissed Mary French, and told her, 'Remember – I love you.' His avowal of love did not prevent her from gradually distancing herself from him and easing herself out of the relationship. Revulsion at what he had done had destroyed the feelings she had for him. But she kept the dreadful secret.

In the following year Charles Schmid became involved with a pretty but neurotic seventeen-year-old named Gretchen Fritz. One evening this girl rang him from her parents' home in California, where she had gone on a visit, and told him that she had 'gone all the way', as she put it, with a man she had met there. Charles sobbed wildly and for days went about like a bear with a sore head, but it was not long afterwards when he told a friend,

The Desert Killer

Richard Bruns, that Gretchen was becoming 'too possessive' …

On 16 August 1965 Gretchen and her thirteen-year-old sister Wendy went to a drive-in movie, from which they returned to the bungalow, and while they were there Charles Schmid strangled both of them and dumped their bodies in the desert. Questioned by two private investigators who had been hired by the girls' parents to find them when they went missing, Schmid insisted that they had told him that they were going to run away to California to join a hippie commune.

However, Charles Schmid was quite unable to resist boasting – it was part of his psychological make-up. He told his friend Richard Bruns that he had killed the two sisters and buried their bodies in the desert, but Bruns did not believe him. 'Aw, who would murder two dames and then blab about it, even to his best buddy?' Bruns said.

But Schmid insisted that he was telling the truth. So Bruns issued a challenge. 'If you buried them, let's go and see the place,' he said, 'right now.' They piled into Schmid's car and Schmid pointed out the shallow graves to his friend. The sand, disturbed by the wind and rain of a recent storm, had uncovered both bodies, still undiscovered in this remote area of the desert.

'So it is true,' Bruns said.

'Of course it's true,' Schmid retorted. 'I wouldn't lie about a thing like that.'

'The guy's crazy,' Bruns thought. 'Stark raving loco.'

'Help me re-bury them properly,' Schmid ordered his friend. He fetched a spade from the trunk of the car, and after the bodies were completely covered, the two young men fetched rocks and scattered them on top. 'Now you're in this as deep as I am,' Schmid told his friend.

In San Diego, Schmid was arrested for harassing young bikini-clad girls on the beach by posing as an FBI agent and asking them questions, but he was let off with a caution. Back at his home in Tucson, he was becoming increasingly tense and edgy, and suffered from increasingly frequent nightmares. He awoke one night screaming, 'I know God is going to punish me!' and drenched in sweat. The four friends who were staying with him at the time found it all they could do to calm him.

Most of the teenagers around Charles Schmid in Tucson seemed to know instinctively that it was he who had killed the three missing teenagers, but none of them dared tell their parents what they knew, nor confide in anyone their suspicions, let alone tell the police. Richard Bruns, observing Schmid's neurotic behaviour, began to fear for his own life; after all, he was the only living witness who could finger him for the murder of the two Fritz girls. His girlfriend, too, could be in danger. Schmid had approached her, and been firmly rejected. Since that time, Bruns had taken to guarding her house at night. Finally, realizing that he could not keep tabs on her house at all times (he had to attend lectures and seminars at his college), he summoned up courage and went to the police, and led them to where the two bodies were buried.

Schmid, who had recently married a fifteen-year-old girl after a blind date, was arrested, and as soon as he was safely in custody John Saunders and Mary French went to the police to tell them about the death of Alleen Rowe at Schmid's hands, and led them to the spot where her body was buried.

The case shocked the conservative parents of Tucson, who had been only dimly aware of how far their children, and their children's associates, had become involved in alcohol, sex and drug abuse. Schmid was sentenced to two terms of life imprisonment, escaping the death penalty only as a result of its suspension in 1971. Mary French received five years in prison as an accessory, and John Saunders was sentenced to life imprisonment.

In 1972 Schmid and another inmate escaped from the Arizona State Prison, but were recaptured a few days later. Richard Bruns, the chief prosecution witness who had been instrumental in Schmid's arrest, was not taking any chances. He married his girlfriend and the couple moved to his parents' farm in Arkansas.

15 The Pressure Cooker Murder

At two o'clock in the morning during the night of 8 May 1968, a woman resident in a block of flats situated along a country road just outside Windsor, in Berkshire, was awakened suddenly by a terrific crash outside. She jumped out of bed and, looking out of the window, she saw in the darkness the dim outline of what appeared to be a car on the opposite side of the road which had mounted the grass verge, crashed through a wooden fence and landed half in and half out of the adjoining field. She telephoned the police and went back to bed.

When a Panda car arrived at the scene, the officers found a coloured man wandering around in the road; he seemed to be in a daze, although apparently uninjured. He gave his name and address, and told the officers that he had dozed off at the wheel of his car which had then careered off the road and gone through the fence and into the field. He had not been drinking and no one had been hurt, so he was allowed to leave. He was driven in a police car to the nearest railway station so that he could catch a train to his home in Harlesden, London, since his car was unusable.

After dropping him off, the sergeant who had driven him to the railway station returned to the scene of the crash to take a more detailed look at the wrecked car. It had been arranged with the driver that the police would tow it to a local garage for repairs, but the officer was curious that there were no keys in the ignition. When he had asked the driver – who had identified himself as Henry Kinch, a native of Barbados – where they were, he had replied that in his dazed state he must have dropped them in the field as he climbed from the wrecked car. It was futile searching for the keys by torchlight in the grass, so the officer made a note to have the area searched thoroughly when daylight came.

The trunk of the car was locked, and without the keys it could not be opened, so the sergeant took out the rear seat of the car so that he could examine the trunk, or at least that part of it accessible from the space left after the removal of the seat. In the trunk he found a cardboard box. On opening it he was horrified to find a human arm, which appeared to be the right arm of an adult black male. Their plans were now hastily changed; forensic experts would have to examine the car before it could be repaired, so the car was towed to the police-station instead of to the garage. The important thing now was to find Kinch and question him.

Kinch, who had given his correct name and address to the officers, had returned to the scene from the railway station, and before long he was picked up and taken in to Windsor police station for questioning as a possible murder suspect. Meanwhile, a Divisional Detective Inspector drove to Kinch's home, together with two other officers, to examine it for any possible evidence of any crime.

Kinch lived in a terraced house let out into single bed-sits, almost all let to West Indians. There were no signs of blood or violence in Kinch's room; in fact, there was nothing at all to arouse the officers' suspicions. The only point of note was that Kinch was, apparently, an avid meat-eater. On the table stood a pressure cooker in which were what looked like four or five pigs' trotters, and on a top shelf in the larder was a large joint, apparently roast beef, already cooked. In the back garden a large stone jar was found, which contained six or seven uncooked meat cutlets. The officers wondered why this meat was in the garden; one suggestion was that since there was no fridge, meat would be cooler outside than in the house.

The officers interrogating Kinch at Windsor discovered that he was a black belt karate expert, a fact which was corroborated by the finding in his room of exercise pads on the walls which the six-foot-six powerfully-built suspect used for practising karate strikes and kicks. No

The Pressure Cooker Murder

evidence of any crime was found at this stage of the investigation.

The Divisional Detective Inspector, with one other officer, drove to Windsor police-station, where Kinch was in the interview room still being interrogated by five or six officers. Up to that point, all that he had admitted to was that he had been driving along when he dozed off and crashed the car. Asked what was in the trunk, he said that he had hired he car and did not know what, if anything, was in the trunk as he had not looked. There were one or two suspicious points, however: a large Bowie knife had been found in his possession, and there were also a number of minute cuts on his fingers, which he claimed had resulted from a job he had had trussing chickens.

Although the suspect made no admissions, the evidence against him was gradually building up, and Sir Keith Simpson, the Home Office pathologist, was called in. Later the same day the trunk of the car was forced open and another cardboard box was discovered similar to the one in which the arm had been found; this second box contained a number of bones. These bore a resemblance to the bones that had been observed in the pressure cooker when the police had examined Kinch's bed-sit in Harlesden. The pressure cooker with its contents, together with the joint from the larder and the stone jar of meat cutlets in the garden, had all been brought to the forensic laboratory. Sir Keith found that the bones in the cardboard box from the car were identical to those in the pressure cooker, and consisted of foot and hand bones with fingers, boiled in a bid to destroy any fingerprints and, equally obviously, to disintegrate the feet so that a shoe size could not be determined. The joint, supposed to have been roast beef, was one of the victim's buttocks, and the stone jar contained a number of assorted body parts. All were human. They were the remains of a middle-aged black male.

The Divisional Detective Inspector was to drive the suspect to Harlesden police station to be formally charged. Up till now, Kinch had made flat denials to all suggestions that he could be involved. After all, he had pointed out, the police did not even know the identity of the man they alleged was the murder victim. Damning evidence had accumulated, including corroboration of various points by neighbours, and the further examination of the house where Kinch had lived, where it was discovered that blood and human tissue still remained in the S-bend and piping of the bath. On being questioned, other tenants in the house described how Kinch had spent two whole days in the kitchen that served the tenants on his floor, boiling pans containing meat for hours, and that a peculiar odour had pervaded the house during that time. A lower jaw, which had disassociated itself from the rest of the head, apparently during the process of boiling, had also been found, wrapped in newspaper, in the hedge near the spot where the car had been wrecked, during a search of the area by the police. It seemed as though a dog had dragged it clear of the thorny growth at the hedge bottom, probably while being taken for a walk; traces of dog saliva and teethmarks were lifted from the newspaper, which had not been unwrapped, so it was presumed that the dog had been on a lead and that its owner had pulled it back to the footpath before it could remove the covering from its unsavoury find. An appeal was put out for anyone who had been walking a dog in the area since the time of the car crash, but no one came forward. The remainder of the head was never found.

The confession which came in the end was unexpected. For the first twenty minutes of the car drive from Windsor to Harlesden, the suspect remained silent. Then the Divisional Detective Inspector decided to play a hunch, based on his long experience of the psychology of suspects. 'Look,' he said, 'once we get to Harlesden we'll be dealing with you in a very formal way. So if I can help you by contacting somebody, ask me now, and I'll do it for you. I'd sooner you asked now rather than later – it would be much more difficult once we're at the police station.'

The DDI's gamble worked. As soon as he had been offered help, Kinch gave way, his composure visibly shaken. Suddenly he broke down, sobbing like a small child. After the paroxysm had abated, he then asked the officer to contact his mother in Barbados and inform her that he was in trouble, and from that point onwards he

The Pressure Cooker Murder

co-operated in every way with the police. On arrival at Harlesden police station, his confession poured forth like a torrent and the whole story came out, revealed in all its sordid horror.

Kinch had stabbed the landlord of the rooming-house to death in the early hours. It appeared that the landlord had just come out of prison and thought that Kinch had been having an affair with his wife while he had been inside. The landlord, it was alleged, had sworn to kill him, but Kinch had decided to 'get in first', as it were. He killed him by stabbing him in the chest with his Bowie knife, and then decided that the best way to dispose of the body would be by cooking it. He had carried the body into the bathroom, cut off the head, arms and legs with a Stanley knife, and drained out all the blood into the bath. He then decided that he had to get rid of any parts which could be used to identify the victim, so he boiled the head, the hands and the feet in the pressure cooker, believing that (to quote his statement) 'they would dissolve and he would be able to throw them away in the garden.'

The remains of the hands could not provide fingerprints, so there was a problem with the formal identification of the body. The victim's wife, however, told the police that her husband had been convicted of robbery as a youth in Barbados, and that he had been sentenced to several lashes with the cat-o'-nine-tails. The scars from the lash marks were still visible on his back, she continued, and she would be able to identify the body from these. She was therefore taken to the mortuary. Since there was no body to speak of – just part of the torso – the police and mortuary assistants arranged it with a cloth draped over both ends so that just the part of the back bearing the scars were exposed to view. This was done as discreetly as possible. The woman took one look and cried, 'Oh, God! – yes, that's him!' and then fainted on the spot.

A new suitcase and a spade, also new, were found among Kinch's possessions, and he readily admitted that he had intended to place the torso in the suitcase, put it in his car and take it out to bury in some remote location. He had already abandoned the story that he had hired the car – it was his own car – and he also admitted that at the time of the car crash he had deliberately 'lost' the keys by flinging them into the hedge. The keys were never found. He insisted, however, that he had not 'staged' the crash – he had genuinely dozed off while driving.

Kinch was charged with the murder of his fellow-Barbadian, and insisted on pleading guilty to murder, against the advice of his solicitor, so that no evidence was ever given in court, and only a few newspapers carried any mention of the case. Most of these reports were inaccurate as they referred to the case as 'the cannibalism murder', whereas Kinch had made it quite clear to the police that he had cooked the body parts purely in order to destroy them and render identification impossible.

Kinch was sentenced to life imprisonment, and he declared at the hearing that if he were paroled or released at some future date it was his intention to return to Barbados.

An interesting sidelight appears from one of the statements submitted by the young constable who had been allotted the job of locating and detaining Kinch for questioning after the arm had been found in the box in the car. Knowing that Kinch had been dropped off by another officer at the railway station, he had gone there in the first instance, and soon learned that no man of the suspect's description had in fact boarded a train, or purchased a ticket in order to travel later. Staff could scarcely have missed him, as he was six feet six inches tall. On the off-chance the young constable had returned to the scene of the car wreck, and had spotted the suspect in the field by the side of the road.

The correct procedure for taking in a suspect, especially one as huge and powerful as Kinch, would have been for the policeman to radio for assistance, and not try to bring him in himself unaided. But the policeman, acting on his own initiative, decided to approach the suspect very casually, with no suggestion that he was going to be arrested, and try to talk him into coming across to the car for a chat about the circumstances of the crash. The young Windsor policeman strode out boldly across the field, approaching the suspect head-on. 'When I was about ten yards from him,' his statement read, 'I shouted out,

The Pressure Cooker Murder

"Kinch, I am a police-officer. Stay where you are. You are suspected of murder." ' The constable had only a truncheon in one hand and a pair of handcuffs in the other, and told him that it was his intention to handcuff him and take him to Windsor police-station. Kinch had made up his mind not to resist; he just stood there, saying nothing. But the outcome could have been very different; with a single karate chop he could have broken the officer's neck. The policeman was a brave man, although he was, of course, not acting 'by the book'.

When he walked up to where the suspect was standing to put on the handcuffs, he found that they were much too small to snap round the huge wrists of this giant of a man. Just at that point back-up arrived, but Kinch offered no resistance. The record is silent on the matter of what action, if any, was taken in regard to the intrepid young copper.

16 The Man who Blew up Trains

The Budapest to Vienna night express, carrying a large number of passengers – businessmen, families returning from their holidays, students returning to university – roared through the Hungarian countryside on 12 September 1931, and at about midnight it reached the Bia–Torbagy Viaduct in the eastern part of Hungary, not far from the Austrian border. As it did so a bomb which had been placed on the viaduct bridge exploded, blowing up the train, which plunged into the gorge below, killing twenty-two people and injuring dozens more, fourteen of them seriously. The carnage was incredible; mutilated bodies lay everywhere, and blood spattered the wreckage in all directions, amid the screams of the injured and the shouts of the rescuers looking for the trapped.

In the next few hours police, firemen, ambulancemen and newspaper reporters converged on the scene. The police were of the opinion that the bomb had been planted by a group of political extremists, but no one claimed responsibility for the outrage. And while police, firemen and ambulancemen toiled to free trapped passengers and to tend the injured and convey them to hospital, the reporters covered the incident for their respective newspapers and in many cases found survivors too shocked and dazed to give them coherent information about the disaster, describe what had happened to them or give any opinions as to the cause. One reporter, however, an Austrian named Hans Habe, had better luck as he was approached by a middle-aged, stockily-built, well-dressed man, who introduced himself as a Hungarian businessman named Sylvester Matushka, who spoke excellent German. This man of his own accord started to talk to him in detail about the crash.

Matushka, a married man with one child, who lived in Vienna, had been staying in Budapest on business. He appeared to have escaped injury completely, and was not in a state of shock, or even nervous; in fact he seemed quite pleased with himself that he had been in a position to give Herr Habe all the information he needed to enable him to write a good story for his paper, which was one of the leading dailies in the capital. Herr Habe, too, was feeling very pleased with himself at having had the luck to secure such a scoop. He gave Matushka a lift back to Vienna in his car.

In Vienna, Matushka provided Herr Habe with plans and drawings of details of the wreckage, and also photographs of himself for publication along with the young journalist's story as the source of his scoop. The newspaper story created a sensation, and made Habe's reputation. Having drawn so much attention to himself, however, Matushka found himself viewed askance by police in both Austria and Hungary, who decided that a little discreet investigation would be in order.

First of all, it was discovered that Matushka had indeed purchased a ticket to travel on the train, but this had not been punched and collected – in other words, Matushka had not travelled on the Bia–Torbagy Express that night. Doubt had arisen as to this on Matushka's suing the railway company for damages for injuries sustained; when the customary medical examination was carried out, the doctor could find nothing wrong with him – not even a cut or a bruise. Matushka explained this by saying that he had dislocated two joints in an arm and a leg, which had 'gone back into place' a few days later, leaving no visible mark or swelling. The medical examiner confirmed that it was for all practical purposes impossible that articular dislocations of the type described could have 'gone back into place' unaided, and that a certain amount of residual swelling, with accompanying bruising, would have remained evident for a longer period than Matushka had claimed.

During the course of the investigation, it was further found that none of the other passengers on the express could remember him, and at that stage it was thought that he had travelled to the scene by car in order to be 'on the spot' so that he could perpetrate a bare-faced fraud. The investigation continued, and a check was made on his background. It was discovered that he had been involved in a number of black market deals and swindles since the 1914–18 war, and that he had recently purchased quantities of dynamite from two different munitions factories. This now put a different light on the events of 12 September 1931. By now the police had enough suspicious evidence to arrest him.

Matushka was questioned not only about the Bia–Torbagy disaster but also about two previous railway explosions earlier that same year. On 8 August the Basle to Berlin express was blown up at Jüterborg, causing many casualties, and earlier an attempt had been made to blow up a train at Ansbach, in southern Austria, but this attempt was bungled and only one carriage derailed, with few passengers injured, none seriously. Curiously, however, Matushka had not appeared talking to reporters or otherwise, and no claims had been put in for compensation. Were the police dealing with a train-wrecking maniac, who had sued the railway after the third crash merely as an afterthought?

The police did not have long to wait to find out. Matushka confessed to all three outrages, triggering the explosions by using a home-made electrical detonating device. Asked why he thought that his attempt to derail the Vienna to Passau express near Ansbach on 1 January 1931 had been a comparative flop, he explained that it had been his first attempt and he had only perfected the technique later. He claimed that train crashes had exerted a powerful influence on him since boyhood, and made the bizarre claim that as a youth he had visited a fair-ground hypnotist, who had imbued him with the spirit of a man called Leo, whose voice he heard in his head, urging him to commit crimes in which many people would die, but he 'had not had the guts', as he put it, to attempt to do so sooner. He claimed no political motive for the bombings, but he did admit to the psychiatrist who examined him that he had had an orgasm at the moment the disaster occurred, in each of the three cases. This established him as a sexual deviate who readily admitted that prior to the bombings he had been able to obtain sexual satisfaction only by imagining train crashes with accompanying sadistic fantasies.

Matushka was sent for trial on 15 June 1932 in Vienna, charged with the attempted derailment at Ansbach. Although the court could accept that he was motivated by sexual lust, they gave no credence to his claims regarding 'Leo' and the voices and the influence of the alleged hypnotist, which they considered a ploy to escape justice by feigning insanity. He was sentenced to six years' hard labour, after which he was extradited to Hungary to be tried for the Bia–Torbagy crime. Asked in court to state his profession, he gave this as 'train-wrecker'. The jury could not agree on a verdict at his first Hungarian trial, and at his second trial he was sentenced to death for the Bia–Torbagy outrage. At these proceedings a map was put into evidence which had been found at his home in Vienna, on which future planned train disaster sites had been marked, including Amsterdam, Marseilles and Paris. This may have been a deciding factor in this second trial.

The death sentence, however, was automatically commuted to one of life imprisonment, since the death penalty did not exist in the country from which he had been extradited, so the train-wrecker had ample time to languish in prison dreaming of disasters which might have been …

It would seem that Matushka remained in prison until Hungary was overrun by the Russians and that he was then freed, but no one seems to know what became of him subsequently. Many sightings were reported, which were probably spurious. Only one thing is certain, and that is, that there were no more train disasters in either Austria or Hungary, or any other European country, which could be attributed to Sylvester Matushka.

17   The Coffin Case

On 5 June 1953 three Americans left their homes in Holidaysburg, Pennsylvania, to spend a fortnight's vacation hunting across the Canadian border in the Gaspé region of Quebec. They travelled in a truck loaded with equipment for shooting game and camping, and were amply provided with all the essentials necessary for survival in the wilderness. The party consisted of Eugene Lindsay, his son Richard, and a companion named Frederick Klaar.

They had told their families that they would be back in approximately fourteen days, give or take the odd day or two, and when they did not return at this time no one was overly concerned because a hunting trip, they knew, could prove so absorbing that they could very easily have decided to extend it to three weeks. However, when four weeks had elapsed and there was still no word from the hunters, anxiety grew about their welfare. They all had jobs to return to, and it was unlike them not to report in for work after a holiday or indeed at any time when they should be at their places of employment, since they all had a reputation for reliability. So, on 5 July, it was decided to report the three men missing to the police. Something must have happened to them: accident, injury or sickness could not be ruled out. Wild animals, including grizzlies, abounded in the area where they had gone hunting. Rattlesnakes infested the forests. They could have suffered a major vehicle breakdown, though this was thought to be unlikely as they had carried ample supplies of spares and two of the party were skilled motor mechanics.

The American police asked the RCMP (Royal Canadian

Mounted Police) to look for them, and gave them details of the area where the three men had said they were going. Their truck was found abandoned near an unoccupied mining prospectors' camp near the St John River, but there was no sign of the occupants. The search was aided by a mining prospector named Wilbert Coffin, aged forty-three, who told the RCMP that he had encountered the three Americans on 10 June and had helped them move their truck which had become stuck in the mud.

Shortly after Coffin had joined the search party, the body of Eugene Lindsay had already been found by another group of searchers at a spot known as Camp 24. The body was lying beside a stream, and had been decapitated. Part of his scalp was found on the opposite bank. The body appeared to have been badly mauled by marauding bears and dragged across the stream by the animals, judging from the state of the dead man's clothes, which had been ripped and shredded by animal claws. A closer examination disclosed bullet holes in the clothing, and his rifle, found nearby, had some of his own head hair on the butt, along with dried blood.

Eugene Lindsay was known to carry large amounts of money on him and when his empty wallet was retrieved the most likely explanation for his death seemed to be that he had been set upon and robbed.

A little later the bodies of Richard Lindsay and Frederick Klaar were found, about two miles away at a spot called Camp 26. They, too, had both been shot, and both bodies subsequently mutilated by bears, which were numerous in the region. The RCMP concluded that Eugene Lindsay had been killed for his money and that his companions had suffered a similar fate because they had witnessed the murder or at least had known the identity of the killer.

Wilbert Coffin, who knew the area intimately, was arrested on suspicion of murder, in what was to become known as one of the most sensational cases in Canadian criminal history. He had admitted meeting the three hunters and had been able to pinpoint the exact location of this meeting, but although he had stated that he had assisted the men dislodge their truck from the mud, no such muddy place could be found at that spot, neither were any logs or other objects used for traction in evidence. The evidence against Coffin was purely circumstantial, and there were several inexplicable anomalies which led to contentious views: many thought it possible that an innocent man had been convicted. Despite his plea of innocence, Coffin's counsel would not allow him to take the stand at his trial and testify on his own behalf, and the only statement he was able to make was an account written in prison after he had been sentenced to death.

According to this, he had seen two other American hunters travelling in a jeep in the vicinity of Lindsay's party and had so informed the RCMP before his arrest. Two independent witnesses, who did not know Wilbert Coffin, were found who had reported seeing a similar vehicle in the area. This lead was followed up and, indeed, after the trial a jeep matching the description of the one seen in the alleged sighting was recovered near the town of Bathurst, having been apparently abandoned. Unfortunately this promising lead was not followed up until *after* Coffin had been sentenced.

There were two sensational developments in the case, one taking place before Coffin's execution and the other after the event. On 6 September 1955 Coffin, having been refused permission to plead before the Supreme Court, broke out of Quebec's City Prison, armed only with an imitation revolver which he had carved from a piece of soap. He went straight to his lawyer, who advised him to return to prison, which he did, but he was refused an appeal for a new trial, despite this having been on his lawyer's instructions, and he was also refused permission to marry his common-law wife, which he had applied to do. He had no fewer than seven stays of execution on various legal and procedural points, and no one could have worked harder to save him than his lawyer. All his efforts, however, came to nothing, and the man whose name was a symbol of death was hanged on 10 February 1956.

On 2 November 1958 police in Miami arrested Francis Gilbert Thompson, a Canadian Indian, who confessed to the murder five years earlier of the three American hunters in Canada. Thompson had been arrested on a vagrancy charge when he made this revelation, and implicated a second man named Johnny Green. The Quebec police were of course notified, but despite Thompson's detailed account of the murders, the court did not believe him and declared him to be an impostor. Thompson maintained that his confession was true for several days, and then, unaccountably, suddenly withdrew it.

It subsequently became known that Eugene Lindsay had a reputation as a money-lender who exacted tough terms from his customers. He frequently carried large wads of money, often two thousand dollars or more, and was certainly a man with enemies. Whoever murdered him and his companions had chosen a very remote location in which to carry out his aim, so as to delay discovery of the bodies and enhance his own chances of escape. Leaving the bodies to marauding bears would make their identification and the cause of death even more difficult to ascertain, and the fact that Eugene Lindsay's head has never been found remains an abiding mystery to this day.

18   A Family Conspiracy

In stark contrast to today's street policing, based mainly on smart black-and-white Panda cars cruising our city thoroughfares and the beat copper with his sophisticated electronic walkie-talkie who can radio for assistance at the push of a button, the Victorian guardian of the Queen's peace had just a truncheon and a whistle at his command to summon assistance. But the ill-lit narrow streets and dark, unlit cobbled alleys of the cities, so well described by Charles Dickens, often had a police patrol watchman who would make the rounds every hour and see that all was well – a system which has much to recommend it in these days of muggings, rapes and nocturnal prowlers looking for vulnerable homes to break into and rob.

The murderer of tiny, ill-nourished six-year-old Barbara Waterhouse had taken a terrible risk of discovery when he had the temerity to dispose of her body by leaving it, bundled into a tattered green shawl, in the cobbled yard of Alexander Street, Leeds, for in those days the police-station for the area was in the Town Hall, a building less than a hundred yards from the ill-lit alley. Furthermore, the alley itself was subject to the hourly scrutiny of Will Ross, the police patrol watchman. And no one but Will Ross himself knew the time at which he would be passing through the cobbled yard; he changed the time every night, so as to discourage the thieves who would otherwise have been able to plan robberies to avoid a regular police timetable.

At 11 p.m. on the night of 10 June 1891 Will Ross had checked the alley, which served as a delivery yard for the municipal offices, and had found nothing suspicious. An hour later, as the chimes of midnight resounded from the clock tower, the constable's lantern illuminated the ghastly bundle as he retraced his footsteps of an hour before. With a policeman's curiosity, he lifted a corner of the shawl, for he thought it was something more than just a bundle of old rags. To his horror, a bloodstained leg protruded from the material – a child's leg. He quickly summoned help from other officers with his whistle, and the shawl with its grisly contents was taken to the police station.

On examination, the body was soon identified as that of Barbara Waterhouse, the daughter of a quarryman named David Waterhouse, who lived in Horsforth, a tiny village outside the city. Barbara had been missing from home since the preceding Saturday. Her throat had been cut from ear to ear, almost severing the head, and she had been stabbed forty-six times. The torso had been savagely ripped from groin to chest, and had been completely drained of blood. She had also been raped before death.

It was a crime to shock not only Leeds but the nation, and to give the murderer the dubious distinction of being the first man to hang in Armley Jail's newly constructed execution shed.

A police constable was despatched on horseback to break the grim news to the parents in the early hours, and the distraught couple caught the first train, at 5.30 a.m., to Leeds in order to provide their formal identification of the body; the police had skilfully arranged it so that only the child's face, carefully washed, was visible in a white shroud, in order to spare the parents' feelings as much as possible.

The police and the public believed that a maniac was at large, yet, as will be shown, at least three persons already knew the identity of the murderer ...

Several hours earlier on the Wednesday night, before the body had been found by Constable Ross, 58-year-old Mrs Ann Turner and her son Walter Lewis Turner, thirty-two, a mill-hand, who lived in Back Lane, Horsforth, had transported the body of the dead child in a tin trunk by train the five miles to Leeds. There they left the trunk at the home of Mrs Turner's deaf and dumb daughter, Mrs Alice Burns, a widow, who was unaware of its contents. Mrs Turner then went on to visit the home of an old friend named Mrs Cotterell, who lived in Portland Crescent. To her she poured out the whole story of her finding the body in the coal-hole at her home on the Monday morning. Mr Cotterell, her friend's husband, told her to take the body to the police. Mrs Turner made some non-committal remark and left, and Mr Cotterell looked anxiously in the following day's newspaper for a report of the crime and, possibly, of the arrest of a murder suspect. Instead, he read of the finding of the body by Constable Ross, but no arrest was mentioned.

Mr Cotterell was angry and alarmed, but he did not wish to become involved personally; however, determined that the murderer of a defenceless child should be brought to justice, he wrote a letter, albeit anonymously, to the Horsforth police, saying that he suspected Walter Turner had murdered the child and urging them to take him into custody. Coincidentally, the Horsforth police had called on Turner in their routine house-to-house inquiries, before they received Cotterell's letter on the Friday. Turner's behaviour had been so suspicious that they arrested him at once, and he was taken to the West Riding County Police Office in Leeds.

Meanwhile, Mrs Turner had decided to confess her part in the murder, and made a statement to Leeds Borough Police, who had not been informed of her son's arrest by their Horsforth colleagues; indeed, they had set out to arrest him five hours after he had already been taken into custody only a few yards from their own headquarters. There seems to have been an astonishing lack of liaison between the region's police forces ...

The trial, at Leeds Assizes in August 1891, drew huge crowds. Mrs Turner appeared in the dock, charged with being an accessory after the fact to murder, and after a whole day in court was sentenced to penal servitude for life. The following day her son appeared in the dock, charged with the murder of Barbara Waterhouse. But before his trial commenced, Mrs Turner was again put up and formally charged with murder, and on the judge's direction was then formally acquitted without any evidence being given. She was then called for the prosecution to give evidence against her son. The court was told that Walter Turner had kept the coal-hole door at their home closed all day on the Sunday following Barbara's disappearance, and that she had discovered the body on the Monday morning when she went to fetch coal to light the wash-house copper. She had then gone out and purchased chloride of lime to sprinkle on the body to prevent any odour. She said that her son, upon being questioned, had told her that a man he did not know had killed the child while he was drunk. Turner, too, had been drunk at the time. Mrs Turner went on to say that the best way of dealing with the matter would be to put the body in a trunk and take it to Leeds, which is what they did, travelling together. After Turner had dumped the body in the yard at Alexander Street, he had taken the trunk to the Midland railway station, leaving it on a platform.

The police had been unable to discover where the murder had actually been committed, and indeed, apart from Mrs Turner's statement about the abandoning of the body in Alexander Street, there would have been no evidence to link Turner with the murder. On the other hand, the defence could not prove an alibi, nor produce any evidence that any man other than Turner himself could have murdered Barbara.

The jury was out for only fifteen minutes, and in sentencing Turner to death Mr Justice Scranton told him: 'This is the most atrocious crime it has ever been my lot to try. Had the people in whose midst this crime was committed ever got hold of you, you would have met death at their hands. Had these people seen, as I saw, the way in which this poor little girl was mutilated, I am afraid that no power of the law, nor all the police in this town of Leeds, could ever have prevented them from tearing you limb from limb.'

Then, as Turner, looking indifferent to his fate, was led below to the cells, the judge called for the victim's mother and presented her with the bouquet which had graced his desk that day. He then left the court to the accompaniment of the cheers of the vast assembly in the court precinct, which continued until his carriage was lost to sight.

A Family Conspiracy

The sensations surrounding this trial, however, were not yet at an end. The following day, back in court, the judge announced that, because he believed that Mrs Turner had acted in good faith purely out of her natural love for her son in trying to conceal the crime, he was reducing her sentence to one of a year's imprisonment.

Walter Turner, who three years previously had been sentenced to nine months in prison for attempting to cut his wife's throat at their home, then in Saltaire, and from whom he was now separated, showed little emotion or regret during his wait for the scaffold. He kept his appointment with the hangman on the morning of 18 August 1891, having slept soundly and eaten a hearty breakfast before walking to the newly-built execution shed. Previous hangings had taken place in the old treadmill house, but the new scaffold had been specially constructed. As the white cap was placed over his head, Turner told Billington, the executioner, 'I don't want that', and went calmly to his death.

His plain wooden coffin was buried in the prison yard with only the prison chaplain and legal witnesses present, in stark contrast to the funeral of his little victim in June, when thousands of people from a wide area travelled to Horsforth for her burial, at which people who had never known her sobbed openly, and strong men wept as they threw flowers into her grave.

19   Spelling was his Undoing

In 1921 Streatham, in London, was a select suburb of residential houses, better-class shops, well-lit streets and equally well-maintained roads. Thirlmere Road was a tree-lined avenue of middle-class dwellings in family occupation. The buses wended their leisurely way to and from Croydon, just as they do today, but there was none of the excessive noise and rush of traffic that characterizes the modern commuter's life.

At No. 21 Thirlmere Road a respectable young woman of thirty-one named Irene May Wilkins lived with her widowed mother. Irene Wilkins, whose deceased father had been a barrister, had served in the Women's Army Auxiliary Corps in the First World War, after which she had taken up a career in catering and had held a post as head cook in a boarding-school with forty boarders. This story unfolds at the time when she felt the need for a change and with it a better salary. She was not averse to going to a school out of her home district, for accommodation was usually provided, and in fact she was hoping to obtain a position in a provincial town. It would make a welcome change from London. She would be able to help her mother more if she had a better salary and would of course come and visit her mother when she had leave. So she put an advertisement in the *Morning Post*, an eminently respectable national daily, seeking a head cook's position in a school, stipulating an annual remuneration of sixty-five pounds and offering the usual references.

Irene did not have long to wait for a response to her advertisement. Before midday on the very same day that it had appeared in the paper – 22 December 1921 – a telegram arrived at her home. Someone had certainly been quick off the mark.

Irene's enthusiasm was probably ill-concealed under her genteel exterior as she told her mother that a prospective employer had already offered her an interview. She showed her mother the telegram, which read as follows:

> Morning Post. Come immediately 4.30 train Waterloo. Bournmouth [sic] Central. Car will meet train. Expence [sic] no object. Urgent. Wood, Beech House.

An educated lady such as Mrs Wilkins, and her equally well-educated daughter, would certainly have noticed the two spelling errors in the telegram, but they undoubtedly ascribed these to the post office clerk who transcribed the telegram as received. What is more remarkable is that neither of them thought to check the name and address given, to see if there was a person named Wood living at a place called Beech House in Bournemouth ...

Irene at once went to the local post office and wired the sender that she would be coming on the stipulated train for the interview then left home to catch it shortly after 3 p.m. At some time the same afternoon after she had left, the telegram she had sent to Bournemouth was returned by the post office to 21 Thirlmere Road, with a note attached stating that there was no such name and address as 'Wood, Beech House' in or near Bournemouth. Mrs Wilkins was mystified by this, but she was not unduly anxious or, indeed, alarmed. Once again, she put it down to some kind of mix-up or incompetence on the part of the Bournemouth post-office clerk. Probably some young girl new at the job, she thought.

The arrangement had been that if she was going to accept the job Irene would send her mother a telegram, but that if it did not suit her she would return home the same evening. When no telegram arrived and the girl did not show up by a late hour, Mrs Wilkins knew that something must be wrong. It was completely out of character for Irene not to keep a promise of this kind – she was much too reliable to take such things lightly.

Going to the police was not a thing Mrs Wilkins liked to do, but she considered that, in the circumstances, she had no choice. So she reported her daughter missing.

The following morning was the day before Christmas Eve, and as a sleepless Mrs Wilkins waited anxiously for news, a labourer out at daybreak walking to work in a desolate spot between Bournemouth and Christchurch, now a built-up area but then open farmland, found the dead body of a young woman, his attention having been attracted by seeing two cows in a field nosing at something lying on the ground. He climbed over a wall and shooed the cows away, and saw that the woman was lying on her back, the head covered with blood, bruised and battered as though by a fist, with swollen eyelids and teeth driven into her lower lip. She had obviously put up a terrific struggle, her arms outflung, her hands also scratched and bloody. Her clothes were pulled up around her waist, and her hips and thighs bore many bruises. After he had recovered from the initial shock, the man made off as fast as he could to the nearest telephone and called the police.

An autopsy was performed the same day, and showed that the dead girl's skull had been penetrated by a heavy blunt instrument in three distinct places, one at the hairline on the forehead, one through the left cheekbone and one on the side of the head near the left ear, which had penetrated the brain. Any one of these three blows alone would have caused death. The dead girl was, however, still *virgo intacta* despite an apparent attempt at criminal assault, which may have been foiled by the murderer having been disturbed.

Searching in the vicinity of the murder scene, the police found the imprints of a vehicle shod with Dunlop Magnum tyres with an unusually deep tread, which had pulled up at a point exactly alongside the place where the body had been found, but on the other side of the wall dividing the road from the field.

Identification of the body as Irene Wilkins was not long in being forthcoming, since her description as a missing woman had been circulated in Bournemouth. And while, in the days that followed, Mrs Wilkins spent her unhappiest Christmas and Irene was buried, police were frantically combing the Bournemouth and Christchurch area for clues. No arrest had been made when, nine days after the finding of the body, Irene's attaché-case, containing her changes of clothes and other personal items for a possible new job, including a folder of references and testimonials, was found where it had been hastily thrown into some rhododendron bushes in Branksome Wood on the outskirts of Bournemouth. It was mildewed and had obviously been lying there for several days, and it confirmed the opinion of Superintendent Garrett, who was in charge of the case, that the murderer was a local man who knew the area like the back of his hand.

The 4.30 train from Waterloo had been due in at 6.45, but had been late and had not arrived until 7.03. To drive a car at a moderate speed from the railway station to the scene of the murder would take approximately ten minutes, so it could fairly be assumed that the murder had taken place between 7.30 and 8.45 p.m. A farm labourer was found who had been strolling along the lane shortly after 8.30 to tether some goats, and had seen the silhouette of an empty car standing with dimmed lights in the lane as he walked both from his cottage and back home again. It is more than possible that it was this man who, all unaware, had interrupted the murderer during his attempted rape and had frightened him off.

The police turned their attention to locating the drivers of all cars which had been in the vicinity of the railway station between 7 and 9 p.m. and, in particular, looking for any vehicles which had Dunlop Magnum deep-tread tyres. During this part of the investigation a witness was found who had been just outside the station and had narrowly avoided being knocked down by a man dressed in a black chauffeur's uniform driving a greenish or greyish car without lights. He particularly remembered that there was a young girl in the passenger seat whom he had already observed on the station platform asking a porter something. He recognized her by a distinctive kind of hat she was wearing – light brown suède with a trimming of red suède threaded through slits in the side, with the ends crossing on the left-hand side. Being interested in cars, he had also noticed that the car was of

Spelling was his Undoing

an unusual shape, with a long sloping hood, and the front lights fitted far more forward than was usual.

When the witness read the girl's description in the following day's newspaper he immediately informed the police, giving a very good description of the car and also of the chauffeur. He had no doubt whatsoever that the girl in the car was the same one he had seen on the platform after the arrival of the train at 7.03.

Two days later the first witness's evidence was corroborated by that of a second witness, a commercial traveller who had also been in the vicinity of the station at the material time. This man had recognized the car as an older-model Mercedes, which had a very long hood and forward-placed front lights. Asked what colour the car was, the witness said that owing to the fact that it was dark and he had only station yard lighting to assist him, he could not put it closer than 'greenish' or 'greyish'. Precisely the same description as that given by the first witness – the police were very thankful for car-spotters (who, of course, have a much more difficult task today owing to the multiplicity of car makes and models). The second witness said that he was pretty sure that there were two people in the car, though he could not be sure as to whether they were a man and a woman. Asked whether he remembered the driver wearing a chauffeur's peaked cap, he said that 'I had not taken that much notice – it was the unusual car I was interested in.'

The police now had a good description of the car, and were also on the lookout for one with Dunlop Magnum deep-tread tyres. They also thought that the man was a local resident with a chauffeur's job. Now, no nearer to a solution despite these good leads, they turned their attention to the telegram which had been sent from Bournemouth to Streatham on 22 December. During this investigation, two other telegrams with similar spelling errors were found. They had been despatched on 17 and 20 December respectively, but the recipients had either not been interested or had been unable to attend the interview offered – thereby probably saving their lives.

In the first of these two telegrams *Bournemouth* had again been spelt without its median '*e*', and the middle '*e*' of advertisement had also been omitted. *'Immediate'* had been spelt *'immidiate'* and *'if'* with two *'f's'*. The word *'expense'* had been spelt with a *'c'* instead of an *'s'* exactly as in the telegram which had been sent to Irene Wilkins. In the second telegram the word *'pleasant'* had been spelt *'plesent'* and again *'Bournemouth'* and *'expense'* were misspelt.

The police realized that this was too much of a coincidence to be just that and nothing more, and now set about tracing the identity of the sender. All the car drivers who were identified as driving cars fitted with Dunlop Magnum deep-tread tyres were asked to write the contents of the three telegrams from dictation, and the results scrutinized for similarities of handwriting as well as the errors in orthography. None of these men's written samples matched the wanted examples.

The police toiled on unremittingly, something in the order of 22,000 documents in the case swelled the files, and weeks ran into months. By April, Superintendent Garrett, desperate to catch the perpetrator of this outrage, went through every one of the stockpiled documents personally. It was during this mammoth task that he came upon a report by a subordinate which had been filed away as irrelevant. It was nothing less than the registration number of the suspect car, which the original witness and his son had seen again on 4 January when catching a train to London; he had scribbled the number in his notebook to inform the police on his return. The number of *that* car irrelevant? One can better conjecture than describe Superintendent Garrett's explosion of wrath towards the unfortunate officer who had put in the report.

Garrett lost no time in tracing the car, registration number LK 7405, a Mercedes, the property of a Mr and Mrs Sutton of Barton Close, Bournemouth, who employed one Thomas Henry Allaway as a chauffeur. During the war this man had been a driver in the RASC (Royal Army Service Corps) and had deserted. After his recapture, he had been posted overseas to drive in France and Germany. He was a married man with one child, and lived in a flat provided by his employer with his family. He was, however, a far from trustworthy employee, and had on several occasions stolen cheques from his employer, forging Mr Sutton's signature, and passed them off to various tradesmen who knew him as the Suttons' chauffeur.

It seems that Allaway became somehow aware of the police interest in him, for he was becoming more and more nervous and uneasy. On Thursday, 20 April, whatever criminal cunning or even common-or-garden intelligence he had seemed to desert him completely as panic set in. Instead of abstracting a cheque or two from Mr Sutton's cheque-book, which could, possibly, have passed unnoticed because Mr Sutton had the foolish habit of never bothering to fill in the counterfoils, Allaway stole the complete cheque-book, cashed some cheques with people he knew, and left his employment without benefit of giving notice. He sent his wife and child to her parents' home in Reading, and fled to London. Garrett was now certain that Allaway was his man, but catching him would be another matter. London was a big place …

On 28 April the London police contacted Garrett with the bad news – they had been unable to locate their quarry in any of his known haunts. So Garrett played a hunch. Allaway was known to be very attached to his child, and could very likely have risked all on an extended visit to his family at his mother-in-law's home. He might well have been lying low there for quite some time. Garrett telephoned the Reading police and asked for their co-operation. The suspect could be arrested on a forgery charge in connection with the cheques; this would suffice to hold him until evidence could be put in to charge him with the murder of Irene Wilkins.

That same evening Allaway was arrested in Reading: Garrett's hunch had paid off. He was walking towards his mother-in-law's house when he caught sight of the waiting policeman, but a passer-by, scenting that something was amiss as the fugitive ran off in the opposite direction, managed to trip him up and jump on him, pinning him to the ground long enough for the policeman to come up and clap the handcuffs on the suspect. One might wonder why only one policeman had been waiting for him. Allaway spent that night in a cell in the police station at Reading, and the next day he was taken back to Bournemouth. It was noted that some betting slips found on him when he was arrested had been made out in the same handwriting as that on the decoy telegrams.

A few days after his arrest Allaway was put into an identification parade with about a dozen other chauffeurs and cabmen all wearing uniform. A newsvendor picked him out as a man who had purchased a copy of the *Morning Post* from him early on 22 December. The two witnesses who had seen his car that evening in the railway station precincts were also called. The first man picked out Allaway without any hesitation, while the second man, although he could not swear to his identification, thought that Allaway was the 'most likely' one. The post office clerk who had been on duty at the time the suspect had sent the telegram to Irene Wilkins was also called. She picked him out unerringly.

The clinching factor came, however, when the suspect was asked to write the contents of the three telegrams from dictation. All the original spelling errors were duplicated without exception and, in addition, the word *'Thirlmere'* was spelt *'Thirlemar'* – the suspect no longer having the benefit of the newspaper advertisement to copy from.

Finally, the guard who had signalled in the train on its late arrival at 7.03 particularly remembered seeing Allaway because he had run forward and asked him if this was indeed the train due in at 6.45 which had left London at 4.30. The same witness who had had the presence of mind to note the car number when seeing it in daylight was asked to pick out the hat Irene Wilkins had been wearing from among more than fifty shown to him. He promptly chose the brown suède hat trimmed with red that the dead girl had worn. Further, a man who knew Allaway had seen him changing a Dunlop Magnum deep-tread tyre from a rear wheel of his Mercedes to a Michelin, following the police announcement in connection with their search for vehicles with Dunlop Magnums.

The trial of Thomas Henry Allaway took place on 3 July 1922 before Mr Justice Avory, who has been described as one of England's greatest and fairest judges. His summing-up was completely unbiased despite the overwhelming evidence put before the jury by the prosecution, against which the prisoner's weak denial and flabby alibi were powerless to save him. Not one mitigating factor was put forth in his favour by the defence, who scrabbled desperately in an attempt to shore up the flimsy framework of their case, watching helplessly as it toppled like a house of cards at a breath of wind.

The all-male jury took only one hour to reach their unanimous verdict of guilty of murder, and Allaway was sentenced to death. He applied for leave to appeal, which was granted, but his appeal was rejected out of hand, and the most strenuous efforts of his counsel, invoking every legal technicality he was able to think of, failed to save him. He was hanged on 22 August 1922.

20   A Man called Smith

A more odious and repugnant con-man and criminal than the man who is the subject of this story has never stood trial in the Old Bailey. There was no question as to his legal sanity, neither can there be any doubt as to his motive, which was cold, calculated greed of the most blatant kind. His victims were girls and women who were gullible enough to fall for his superficial charm and plausible promises. A thin veneer of top-hatted, frock-coated pseudo-respectability cloaked his essentially uncouth personality which, as we shall see, frequently broke through in unguarded moments, betraying the soulless avarice which was his dominating passion. The name of this man was George Joseph Smith.

Smith was born at 92 Roman Road, Bethnal Green in London's East End, on 11 January 1872, the son of an insurance agent. By the age of eight he had already been sent to a reformatory in Gravesend, Kent, as being incorrigible and the author of many petty larcenies and other juvenile misdemeanours. On his release at the age of sixteen he returned to his mother, who did not have to look after him for long periods because of his frequent spells in prison for thieving. Then, when he was eighteen, he enlisted in the Northamptonshire Regiment, in which he spent three years without, apparently, getting into trouble.

Smith, however, was irresistibly drawn to crime as a moth to a candle flame. This time, however, he decided to get someone else to do his dirty work for him, by persuading a young woman to steal from her employers. He was soon apprehended and received a year's jail for larceny and receiving stolen goods. He was released in

1897 and went to Leicester, changing his name to George Love. Unfortunately the leopard had not changed its spots. He persuaded a young girl to steal a cash box from her employer, and with the £115 so obtained he opened a baker's shop at 28 Russell Square, Leicester.

On 17 January 1898 he married the eighteen-year-old daughter of a shoemaker. This girl, Caroline Beatrice Thornhill, was his only legal wife among the plethora of bigamous ones he acquired during his loathsome career in the dedicated pursuit of gain. Her father disliked Smith on sight, but somehow she managed to persuade him that she was determined to marry the man she loved. Later she was to say of her husband: 'During the time I knew him, I never knew him do any work ... He had an extraordinary power. The power lay in his eyes ... When he looked at you, you felt that you were being hypnotised. They were small, dark eyes that seemed to rob you of your will.'

This physical magnetism was undoubtedly the secret of his masterful power over women. He was able to persuade even the most genteel and well-brought-up girls to abandon themselves to him body and soul, even within the space of a few days; even older women were not immune to the animal magnetism of this vulgar and semi-literate rogue. There is no other possible explanation for the facility with which he was able to make them his slaves with nothing more than a look or a word, heedless of the consequences to themselves ...

Caroline, whose married name of Love did not invalidate her marriage, moved with her husband back to London shortly after their marriage, Smith having sold the shop, which had proved unprofitable. Smith was not a man to hang on to anything which was not what we would today call a viable proposition, as we shall see. Averse to doing an honest job of work himself, he found jobs in service for his wife, first in London and later in Brighton, Hove and Hastings. Smith seemed to have a particular fascination for the seaside. The object of his wife's jobs was to enable her to steal valuables from her employers, which was fairly easy for her to do as a maid. In Hastings, in the autumn of 1899, she was arrested in a pawnbroker's shop where she was attempting to sell some silver spoons. After twelve months in prison she located Smith and informed on him to the police, resulting in a two-year sentence for her husband meted out in court on 9 January 1901. The sentence was for receiving stolen goods. A wry comment was made after the trial by a local newspaper reporter, who wrote: 'For his spooning at Hastings Love has gone to prison.'

In 1903 Smith, released once more, went looking for the wife who had 'shopped' him, threatening dire consequences, and to escape his clutches she emigrated to Canada and adopted a new name. They were never divorced, so all Smith's subsequent marriages were bigamous.

Smith now returned to London and went back to the middle-aged boarding-house keeper with whom he had stayed before he had moved to the seaside. She must have been very pleased to see him again, for within a few weeks they were married. This was the signal for Smith to bleed her of every penny she possessed – albeit willingly given – and as soon as the unfortunate woman had no more savings or valuables to part with he walked out without so much as a good-bye. Smith now decided to concentrate whole-heartedly on this new and easy method of enjoying all life had to offer without doing a stroke of work – woo 'em, wed 'em and walk right out of their lives with everything they had.

He was cunning enough, of course, to choose a different location for each of his schemes. The seaside towns of the southern coast of England drew him like a magnet, and he spent his time travelling about staying at various seaside boarding-houses and striking up friendships with susceptible young women. Little is known of his activities until 1908, when, in June, he met a widow in Worthing, Mrs Florence Wilson. After a whirlwind courtship, lasting all of three weeks, he swept her off to London, where they went through a form of marriage and he charmed his bride into handing him the modest sum of thirty pounds she had in her post-office savings account, all the money she had in the world.

He dispensed with a honeymoon, telling her that they were a waste of money and that they could just as easily get to know one another better at home – a furnished room. Instead, he took her to see the Franco–British Exhibition at the White City in London, and while they were there he told his unsuspecting new wife that he was just going to nip to Stand 32 to buy a newspaper. After waiting an hour and wondering what could possibly have held him up, she went to look for him. She found that Stand 32 did not sell newspapers but was a display of carpet manufacturers' latest styles. She then thought that the best thing to do would be to go home to their new lodgings, in Camden Town. As soon as she opened the door to their room, she was horrified to find it empty. Smith had vanished with all her furniture, linen and other belongings.

Twenty-seven days later, Smith married Edith Mabel Pegler in Bristol under his real name. Posing as an antique dealer, he moved with her to Bedford, Luton, Croydon, London and Southend. Although no doubt Edith longed for a more settled life with her husband, she accepted this wandering existence without question, out of her love and loyalty, and it must be said that all the evidence shows that Edith was the only woman for whom Smith ever showed some semblance of affection. He would disappear for weeks, sometimes months at a time 'on business', giving various plausible reasons for his long absences. He would send her the odd postcard or letter, occasionally a pound or two. Sometimes he said he had been concluding an antiques deal in Canada or Spain. She trusted him implicitly, and never dreamed that he was 'marrying' other women and fleecing them of their assets. But always he returned to her in the end, and never once was he known to harm her. When she ran out of money, she just took off for her mother's home in Bristol, where he would come and pick her up after a successful 'business deal'.

In October 1909 he married a spinster named Sarah Freeman, who worked as a clerk in Southampton. He said that he had a wealthy relative who had recently died and that he was awaiting a legacy from the solicitors who were dealing with the will. He had married Miss Freeman in the name of George Rose, and after the wedding persuaded his bride to draw out her savings to tide him over until the

A Man called Smith

legacy was forthcoming. He told her that he was going to purchase a shop with a flat above it and start an antique business and would make her manageress so that she could leave her humble clerking job. He took lodgings in London – temporarily, he said – and she withdrew all her post office savings and also cashed in some Government stock. After he had this money in his hands, he took her for a day out, ending in the National Gallery, on 5 November. He asked her to sit and wait for him on a form while he visited the lavatory, but he never returned. Instead he took a bus to Clapham to their lodgings and vanished with all her belongings.

With his ill-gotten gains of about £400 he travelled to Bristol to scoop up the faithful Edith Pegler and then on to Southend, where he established a second-hand furniture shop which he purchased for £270 with £30 remaining on mortgage. He then sold it and the couple returned to Bristol, where Smith purchased 86 Ashley Down Road, paying a small deposit with the rest on mortgage.

Smith, however, was still not satisfied with being a property owner and property dealer. The dreadful pattern repeated itself in one form or another, and it would be wearisomely repetitious to describe all his exploits in similar vein. Indeed, it is thought that many women were too embarrassed and ashamed to inform on him, and preferred to suffer in silence, having learned their lesson the hard way ...

In August 1910 Smith met Beatrice Constance Annie Mundy, who at thirty-one was still unmarried. Her father, who had died in 1904, had been a bank manager and had left her well provided for, with £2500 in gilt-edged securities. This was managed for her in a family trust by her uncle, who allowed her an income of eight pounds a month. It seems that her uncle considered his niece no competent judge of money matters, and, as it later transpired, she was no competent judge of character either ...

One day Beatrice met a self-styled antique picture-restorer who told her that his name was Henry Williams. In a matter of days they were firm friends, and she had confided in him about her financial affairs. Interest of £135 had accrued, she told him, which was in excess of the monthly allowance of eight pounds which her uncle allowed her. 'He thinks I can't handle money!' she told him. 'Never mind,' Smith thought to himself with grim satisfaction, 'I will handle it for her and relieve her uncle of the responsibility. I'll have to marry her first, of course. The girl's no oil painting, but £2500 will be well worth it.'

Only a few days later the two were on their way to Weymouth, where they took lodgings at 14 Rodwell Avenue, and 'married' at the registry office on 26 August. Bessie, as Beatrice was known, wrote an enthusiastic letter to her family, including her uncle, with the news of her wedding. This came as a complete surprise to them, and not to put too fine a point on it, they were distinctly less than enthusiastic. 'Dear Uncle', she wrote, 'I got married today! My husband is writing tonight.' (a foregone conclusion – she was merely paving the way) and continued with fulsome effusions about her new husband. She then signed herself with a flourish, 'Bessie Williams'.

The inevitable letter followed with its ill-spelt demands. 'My wife hopes you will forward as much money as possible at your earliest by registered letter. I am pleased to say Bessie is in perfect health, and we are both looking forward to a bright and happy future. Believe me, Yours faithfully, Henry Williams.'

Smith had to wait, chafing with visible impatience, until 13 December before he could legally receive the £135 interest which had accrued on his wife's securities. As soon as he obtained this money he absconded, realizing that he could not receive the capital. The trust fund had seen to that. But this mean-minded low scoundrel not only took his wife's clothing, but also left her a letter accusing her of having given him a venereal disease – an accusation which was, of course, as groundless as it was heartless and cruel.

One would have thought that the hapless Bessie would have considered herself well rid of her 'husband' and decided to cut her losses. But fate decreed otherwise. For eighteen months Smith resumed his predatory travels, after first going straight to Edith Pegler in Bristol after his latest coup. He opened more antique shops and sold them, financed no doubt by the misfortunes of other too-trusting maiden ladies. Early in 1912 he was back in Bristol with the faithful Edith, but funds were running low, and he told Edith that he was going to do a few deals in the southern counties and then buy some more properties. One of the first places he chose was Weston-super-Mare in Somerset, where, by one of the strangest possible coincidences, Bessie Mundy had chosen to spend her annual seaside holiday. And whom should she meet on the promenade but her errant husband, Henry Williams?

Despite the abominable manner in which he had treated her, despite the fact that she had neither seen nor heard from him for eighteen months, all was forgiven by this foolish and romantic woman under the influence of the hypnotic eyes. 'Let us forget the past', she said, 'and I know we can be happy from now on.' She had no notion of what had made her husband behave in that inexplicable way, nor did she wish to know. Some things were not to be stirred up. Having arranged to meet Smith again later that afternoon, she hurried back to her holiday boarding-house landlady, Mrs Sarah Tuckett, with the flowers Smith had given her. Full of excitement, she related her meeting with her long-lost husband, and asked Mrs Tuckett if she could invite him to tea, as they were going to discuss getting back together. The landlady agreed.

Unlike the women who had been duped by the plausible Smith, Mrs Tuckett took an instant dislike to him when he arrived at the house at 3 p.m. As she was to say later: 'Mrs Williams was very excited that she had found her husband again, but I asked him: how was it that he had left her eighteen months before in Weymouth? He replied that he had been looking for her for more than twelve months and realized that he had been foolish to leave her. I told him that he knew her family's address and could have written to them for her address at any time ... Mrs Williams said she had definitely decided to return to her husband, and she left with him that same night. I never saw her again.'

Smith was equally anxious to remain with the foolish

Bessie. Always the untouchable £2500 was in his mind, and he travelled around, ostensibly on business, while he made official enquiries as to how he could legally obtain possession of the money. He found a solicitor in a town where he was not known, who told him that there was only one way: he and his wife should each make a will leaving everything to the surviving spouse, and that if his wife died first he would be legally entitled to the money. From that moment, the evil seed was sown in Smith's mind, and Bessie's fate was sealed.

Herne Bay in Kent was the town chosen where Smith would rent a house and, he told his wife, they would settle down and he would resume the antique picture-restoring business. He paid a month's rent on a small house at 80 High Street, and had a brass plate affixed to the front door which stated simply, 'Henry Williams, Art Dealer'. Funds were, however, running out because he had been unable to sell an investment property he had bought in Southend and the mortgagees were pressing him for repayment; he had tried to pressure Bessie's uncle into paying him some arrears of interest owing to her, so far without result, and Bessie's monthly allowance of eight pounds did not go very far. He was now desperate. Above all, he was apprehensive that his wife's family would change the terms of the settlement under which she received her income. He must act fast, if the fortune were not to slip from his grasp. So he arranged, on 8 July, for them both to call upon a local solicitor and exchange wills, which the solicitor drew up, in which each spouse left everything to the other. The solicitor was also provided with a copy of Bessie's trust deed.

Bessie was also told by Smith to tell the solicitor that she wanted the trust revoked so that she and her husband could have the use of the capital since they were now married. The solicitor, however, said that counsel's opinion would have to be sought on such a point, and pointed out that the trustees would be most unlikely to consent to any revocation of the settlement. Smith was visibly impatient at the delay involved in having to wait for counsel's opinion to be received. In the meantime, the solicitor had informed him that under the Statute of

Distributions he would receive nothing if his wife died intestate as her estate would go to the next of kin, but if she made a will in his favour it would be a different matter.

The wills having been exchanged and lodged with the solicitor, the couple left the office, Bessie smiling happily up into the face of her husband as she was led like a lamb to the slaughter. Smith smiled back, but his smile was one of grim satisfaction rather than marital happiness. His mind was now made up ...

The following day Smith, wasting no more time, went to an ironmonger's shop and bought a zinc bath, without taps, for one pound, seventeen and six. He had haggled over its original price of two pounds and obtained the reduction as a discount for cash. He even begrudged this spending, for a few days later he returned the bath to the ironmonger's, its grim purpose accomplished, for a full refund.

The next day, 10 July, he took Bessie to a doctor's, telling him that she had had a fit. All Bessie had complained of was a headache, but she was a very compliant woman and did not argue. The doctor gave her some powders. Then, on the 12th, Smith called him to the house, where he found 'Mrs Williams' in bed. Smith had said she had had another fit, although all Bessie could remember was a sleepless night owing to the heat. The doctor found her hot and flushed, but otherwise could find nothing more amiss, and prescribed a sedative, as before. That night Bessie – obviously feeling much better – dutifully wrote a letter to her uncle, describing the 'fit' she was supposed to have had at length, praising her husband for his tender loving care, and referring to the doctor who had attended her as 'the best medical man in town'.

The next morning, at about 7.30 a.m., Smith told Bessie that a bath would do her good 'in her present state of health' although, despite her alleged frailty, he made no offer to fill it for her and left her to make the twenty or so trips up the stairs from the kitchen with buckets of hot water. She got into the bath, her hair in curlers, and a little later Smith went out to buy some fish.

At 8 a.m. a note reached the doctor who had attended

Bessie as he was dressing. 'Can you come at once? I am afraid my wife is dead.' The note was signed H. Williams, 80 High Street. Dr French, a newly qualified young practitioner, hurried to the house without delay. There he found 'Mrs Williams' lying on her back in the bath, her head under water. A tablet of soap was clutched in her right hand. Artificial respiration was attempted, but it was too late.

Dr French left the house to inform the coroner of the fatality and also the police, and at ten o'clock Police Constable Kitchingham arrived to take a statement from the bereaved husband. The unfortunate Bessie lay on the floor beside the bath, stark-naked, and her body was still there at four o'clock when a woman came to lay the body out for burial. The coroner had meanwhile arranged for the inquest to be held on the afternoon of Monday, 15 July.

Smith wired Bessie's uncle: 'Bessie died in fit this morning. Letter following'. The letter commenced: 'Dear Sir, Words cannot describe the great shock I suffered in the loss of my wife. The doctor said she had a fit in the bath ...'

Both her uncle and her brother sent letters to the coroner demanding a post-mortem, but the coroner ruled that this was unnecessary, and the inquest found a verdict of 'death by misadventure'. The only witnesses were called were Smith – who wept copiously throughout the proceedings – and Dr French. The cause of death was given as drowning caused by an epileptic seizure in the bath. It should perhaps here be pointed out that the coroner was a lawyer with no medical knowledge.

Smith had his bride buried in a common grave at 2.30 p.m. the following day, before any of her relatives could get to Herne Bay to attend the funeral. Her uncle lived in Wiltshire and her brother in Dorset. Only a week had elapsed since the wills had been drawn up by the solicitor, signed and witnessed. Before hastening to rejoin Edith Pegler in Bristol, however, there was now the matter of the legacy to attend to. The family vigorously contested the will, but were legally powerless to oppose the due process of law, in that 'Henry Williams' was the sole legatee and that the entire estate of £2500 would go to him – which it did. He opened several bank accounts, purchased seven houses in Bristol, and an annuity for himself.

Until the summer of 1913 Smith and Edith were again on the move, taking in Margate, Tunbridge Wells and other southern towns while he made various 'business deals' which stopped short of murder. Then, Edith having been left once more with her mother in Bristol, Smith decided to explore the possibilities of Southsea, in Hampshire. Here he met a young nurse, 25-year-old Alice Burnham, the daughter of a market gardener. Currently she was engaged as a private nurse to an elderly invalid. She had a little money of her own, partly derived from a family legacy and partly from her own accrued savings.

Miss Burnham fell under Smith's evil hypnotic spell and an engagement quickly followed. Introduced to her father, Charles Burnham, Smith impressed him as a thoroughly repellent and coarse character, but there was nothing Burnham could do to stop his daughter from marrying him – she was, after all, of age. The marriage took place on 4 November in Portsmouth, Smith using his real name for a change. He described himself as a bachelor of independent means.

As may well be imagined, the very first letter Smith wrote to his father-in-law was a demand for money. This was for the return of a loan of £104 which Alice had made to her father. Burnham distrusted Smith and tried to delay sending the cheque, but after a good deal of acrimonious correspondence it was eventually forthcoming at the end of November. In the meantime Smith had persuaded his bride to hand over to him 'for safe keeping' the £27.9.5 which she had in her post office account. He also insured her life for £500 and paid the first premium, and took her to a solicitor to make a will in his favour. The record does not state whether on this occasion he also made a will in *her* favour ...

After this demand for the repayment of the loan had been met, Mr Burnham, disillusioned with his new son-in-law, had engaged a solicitor to try to inquire about Smith's background. When word reached Smith about this, it prompted him to write an abusive postcard to his father-in-law, revealing all his basic vulgarity. The postcard read as follows:

> 'Sir, In answer to your application concerning my parentage, etc. My mother was a Buss-horse, my father a cab-driver, my sister a rough-rider over the arctic regions, and my brothers were all gallant sailors on a steamroller ...

Smith's mind was now assessing the gains he had yet to come from his latest venture into matrimony. Alice had £140 in capital, plus a few pieces of good jewellery and some furniture, linen and so on. There would also be the insurance money in due course ... Smith decided that an out-of-season seaside holiday would not be amiss, although it was chilly and foggy December. So, on the 10th of that month, the couple departed for Blackpool. 'A sort of short honeymoon,' explained the man who had, in a similar previous situation, averred that honeymoons were a waste of time.

Smith, having gained enormous confidence from the success of his last venture, did not rent a vacant house but took rooms with a Mrs Crossley at 16 Regent Road, having refused the one previously viewed in Adelaide Street because it had no bathroom. Mrs Crossley's house did. Smith paid the week's rent of ten shillings in advance. The procedure now took a familiar turn. A doctor was consulted about the headaches from which Alice was suffering – or so her husband said. She was then persuaded to write to her parents, describing her husband in glowing terms, and referring to a mysterious series of headaches which necessitated a doctor's attention: 'I have the best husband in the world,' she wrote, 'and he has engaged one of the area's most eminent specialists to attend me.'

On Friday evening, 12 December, the couple went out for a walk, after Smith had asked their landlady's daughter to prepare a bath for his wife. They returned just after eight o'clock. The new lodgers went upstairs, while the Crossleys sat down to supper in the kitchen. They heard nothing unusual, but about a quarter of an hour later they observed a patch of water coming through the ceiling and down one wall. It seemed that the bath had overflowed; the bathroom was situated above the kitchen. Just then Smith appeared at the kitchen door holding two eggs in his hand. He seemed out of breath, as though he had been hurrying. 'I've brought these eggs for our breakfast tomorrow morning,' he said, handing them to his landlady. She pointed to the ceiling. 'Looks like the bath has overflowed,' she said. 'You had better go and look.'

Smith went upstairs with alacrity, and a few moments later called down from the landing. 'Fetch the doctor! My wife cannot speak to me!'

Dr Billings, the doctor who had attended Alice for her alleged headaches, was sent for, and examined the unfortunate woman, who was still in the bath with her face under water when he arrived; it seemed her husband had not made the slightest effort to remove her or attempt resuscitation. Dr Billings considered this rather odd, but said nothing at the time. He quickly pronounced Mrs Smith dead from drowning, but this time he did not go along with Smith's tentative suggestion: 'You do not think she had a fit, do you?' 'No,' the doctor replied, 'I don't think so.' The inference was that she must have fainted.

Although the Crossley family were deeply shocked that a death – and of a comparative stranger at that – should have occurred in their house, they were even more shocked by Smith's callous attitude afterwards. Alice had died on Friday and the inquest had been arranged for the following day, recording the same verdict as that on the unfortunate Bessie Mundy – death by misadventure, from drowning in the bath. Without letting the Burnham family know at this stage, Smith hastily arranged for a burial in a common grave – 'the kind they put anybody in', as he termed it – on the Monday, and when this was commented upon by Mr Crossley, Smith replied, 'When they are dead, they are dead.' Mrs Crossley could not believe what in her heart she suspected, but the whole thing was too much for her and she told Smith to go. He took a room next-door. She was forced to see him again when he came with the undertaker, who brought the cheapest possible type of coffin. She remonstrated with Smith asking him why he could not at least have ordered a deal coffin. His reply was, 'When they are dead, they are done for.' Mrs Crossley dissolved into tears at the callousness of the man.

Immediately after the funeral Smith left for Southsea, walking to the railway station to save the bus fare. 'We haven't seen the last of him,' Mrs Crossley remarked to her husband over the tea-table that day. 'You mark my words.' Prophetically, she was right.

Only after selling all Alice's belongings which had been moved to the Southsea lodgings did Smith inform her family of her untimely demise, collect the £500 due to him under the insurance policy, and then return post-haste to the waiting Edith Pegler in Bristol. He increased his annuity, made some more property deals, and the couple then once again set out on their travels, visiting London, Cheltenham, Torquay, Bournemouth and other places. When the First World War broke out in 1914, they were staying in Ashley Road, Bournemouth. 'While we were there,' Edith said later, 'my husband was out quite a lot in the evenings, and in the middle of September 1914 he said he would have to go to London for a few days on business.'

The 'business' was the wooing and winning of another 'bride', a maid-servant named Alice Reavil. Cutting a dashing figure in white flannels and a straw boater, he met her as she sat in Battersea Park listening to the band. To cut a long story short, they were married by special licence in Woolwich – on this occasion Smith gave his name as Charles Oliver James and gave his occupation as antique dealer – and went to live in lodgings in Battersea Rise. He was disgusted to find that she was not worth very much financially – certainly not enough to risk murder for – so he took her for a tram ride to Brockwell Park, where he left her waiting for him while he went into a public lavatory by one entrance and out at another, never to return. While the girl sat twiddling her thumbs, he hotfooted it to their lodgings, took ninety pounds – her entire savings – which she kept in a tin box in the wardrobe and had been foolish enough to tell him about, sold her furniture and other items to a second-hand dealer in the same street, and disappeared. Some of her clothes he gave to Edith Pegler, explaining that 'his business deal had included a quantity of ladies' clothing'.

While Edith was enthusing over what was (for him) his generous gift of silks, laces, hats and dresses, Smith announced that he was off again to clinch one of his 'deals'. He had suddenly remembered a lady (with potential) he had met in – of all places – Bath, in Somerset, and he decided to pay her a visit to sound her out.

Margaret Lofty, a spinster of thirty-eight, was the daughter of a clergyman who had died some years before. She took occasional sporadic employment as a lady's companion, and lived with her aged mother and invalid sister. Earlier in the year she had become engaged, but discovered, fortunately just in time, that her fiancé was a married man. She had been unsettled by this disappointment of all her hopes and the futility of her love, and was vulnerable to Smith's blandishments in consequence. What she did not know, of course, was that in relinquishing a man who had been married once, she would be substituting one who had been married several times, and whose first marriage was still legal and binding despite his wife being in Canada. But, as they say, love is blind, and Margaret Lofty was no exception to the genre of women who allow their heart to rule their head.

On 17 December, without informing any of her family, she married Smith, this time calling himself John Lloyd and giving his occupation as estate agent, at the registry office in Bath. The same day they left for London, ostensibly for their honeymoon, and took rooms in Highgate, at 14 Bismarck Road. The house was furnished with a bath ...

The now familiar scenario was enacted with dreary repetitiousness. First of all 'Mrs Lloyd' was taken to see Dr Bates, though in this instance it is not very clear what her complaint was alleged to be. Next, she was persuaded to break the news of her marriage to her family, mentioning her so-called 'ill-health', the solicitude of her new husband and the glowing tribute to the local physician. In her letter to her mother she described her husband as a 'thorough Christian man' and said that she had 'every proof of his love for me ... He has been honourable and kept his word to me in everything ... He is such a nice man.' One can feel only pity for the poor dupe who had fallen into the clutches of this loathsome creature.

As soon as Smith discovered that Margaret Lofty was worth very little financially, he at once set about insuring her life for £700 and without more ado went through the usual procedure of visiting a solicitor and persuading her to make a will in his favour. Hardly had this been signed, sealed and delivered before Smith put in motion his nefarious scheme which has come to be the classic example of 'system' in British criminal history. He had already wheedled from her the only money she possessed – nineteen pounds – on some pretext or other; he could scarcely wait for the proceeds of her life insurance to fall into his hands.

At about 8 p.m. on the night of Friday, 18 December, 'Mrs Lloyd' took a bath. Again, the bathroom was situated above the kitchen, although it did not overflow this time. The landlady, Miss Louisa Blatch, was ironing in the kitchen shortly after this time when she heard sounds emanating from the bathroom. As she was later to say, 'It was a sound of splashing. Then there was a noise, like someone putting wet hands or arms on the side of the bath. Then there was a sort of sigh ...'

Moments after this she heard Smith in the front parlour playing the harmonium – it seemed the monster had a penchant for music – and with sublime hypocrisy he had chosen to play the hymn 'Nearer, my God, to Thee'. About ten minutes later, the front doorbell rang. It was 'Mr Lloyd'. 'I forgot I had a key – sorry to have troubled you,' he said. 'I have been to get some tomatoes for Mrs Lloyd's supper. Is she down yet?' 'No, she isn't,' Miss Blatch replied. 'I haven't heard her about at all. Perhaps you'd better go up and see that she is all right.' No sooner said than done. Moments later, Smith was on the landing, predictably calling for Dr Bates to be sent for. His wife, apparently, had fainted in the bath ...

The inquest was held on 1 January 1915, and Margaret 'Lloyd' was buried on 21 December 1914 – a reversal of the usual procedure. On 4 January Smith called on a solicitor, a Mr Davies, at 60 Uxbridge Road, and instructed him to prove Mrs Lloyd's will and call in the insurance policy moneys. However, this time his luck was to run out. The story of her death appeared in the *News of the World* under the heading 'Bride's Tragic Fate on Day after Wedding' – Smith had speeded up the despatch of his bride since the two previous occasions – and who should read the *News of the World* over breakfast that Sunday but Mr Charles Burnham and Mrs Crossley? Both were immediately struck by the similarities between the death of Mrs Lloyd with those of Alice Burnham and Bessie Mundy. Both went to the local police with their suspicions, and these were in each case communicated to Scotland Yard.

While Smith was waiting for the money to come in, the police were pursuing inquiries that took them to Herne Bay and Blackpool as well as to other towns all over southern England. And when Smith returned to his solicitor on 1 February to collect the money, he was detained as he left the office by Detective Inspector Neil and two police sergeants, on a holding charge of bigamy. He admitted having married Alice Burnham while legally married to Caroline Thornhill. He heaved an inward sigh of relief: 'Oh, it's only for bigamy they want me. I'll get two years at the most.' He could not have been more wrong.

The trial of George Joseph Smith opened at the Old Bailey on 22 June 1915 before Mr Justice Scrutton, when he was charged with the murder of Beatrice Mundy. He had already been charged at Bow Street with the murders of Alice Burnham and Margaret Lofty. In these preliminary hearings he had shouted abuse at lawyers and witnesses, a pattern which was to repeat itself at his trial. The 43-year-old defendant was prosecuted by the senior Treasury Counsel, Mr Archibald Bodkin, assisted by Mr Travers Humphreys. Smith was defended by the great Edward Marshall Hall, with Mr Montague Shearman as his junior. Despite the temperature of more than eighty degrees in July in London, women packed the courtroom, eager for a glimpse of the infamous killer with his hypnotic eyes, apparently unaffected by his vulgar and abusive outbursts. More women who could not gain admission queued outside, in case one who had a seat fainted from the heat and she could take her place.

The trial lasted until 1 July; 112 witnesses were called, and 264 exhibits were entered. At one point the jury were taken into an antechamber, where Detective Inspector Neil demonstrated how the murders must have been committed, using the original bath in which Bessie Mundy had died, and a nurse wearing a bathing-costume. The murderer probably passed his arm under the knees of the woman, most likely in a purportedly playful manner in order to avoid giving her the impression that it was anything more than a bit of fun. Then he lifted her legs with a sudden movement as high as he could, which would have the effect of her head sliding under the water and becoming completely submerged. Water would rush into her air passages and she would become unconscious in seconds, in some cases immediately, and in less than a minute the victim could, and most probably would, be dead. This was amply demonstrated by the nurse losing consciousness almost immediately, having to be pulled out fast and requiring artificial respiration. Unlike three of Smith's victims, she lived to tell the tale.

The bodies of all three victims had been exhumed, and Sir Bernard Spilsbury, the most famous pathologist of them all, gave lengthy descriptions in evidence. After a good deal of legal argument, evidence of 'system' was allowed – a precedent which Mr Justice Scrutton was powerless to prevent. After all, every man and woman in Britain who read newspapers must have felt convinced by now, if not before, that if Smith had murdered any one of the three he must have murdered them all. Accounts of the case had very nearly succeeded in edging the war news right off the front pages. For the judge to tell the jury, as he attempted to do, that Smith was being tried only for the murder of Beatrice Mundy and that they should not allow themselves to be influenced by details concerning the other two cases, was clearly little more than a farce, considering how much evidence had already been put in regarding the deaths of Alice Burnham and Margaret Lofty. Marshall Hall protested, but was overruled, and the admission of system in this case was officially sanctioned.

Once this point was established, more than a hundred witnesses were examined about the events in Herne Bay, Blackpool and Highgate, and Spilsbury, with his assistant pathologist William Willcox, were called to prove that all three victims died from drowning in similar circumstances. No evidence of organic disease was found in the bodies of Bessie Mundy or Margaret Lofty, and in the case of Alice Burnham they had found only a slight thickening of the mitral valve of the heart which would not have affected her health in any way – this condition is almost an everyday occurrence in the autopsies on apparently perfectly healthy persons of any age.

Regarding Dr French's diagnosis of an epileptic fit in the case of Bessie Mundy, this was discredited at the outset. Not only was there no sign of epilepsy on examination of the brain at the autopsy nor any history of the disease in her family physician's record, but it was pointed out that the first effect of the onset of an epileptic fit would be to stiffen and extend the body. Bessie Mundy had been five feet seven inches tall, and the bath was only five feet long. The stiffening and extension of her legs would have pushed her head up out of the water, not down into it, had she suffered such a fit. Asked whether the victim could have become submerged while kneeling or standing in the bath in the event of her having fainted, Spilsbury replied that in such an event she would have fallen forward on her face, in which case she might easily drown. But, he pointed out, she was found dead *face upwards* under the water.

The result of the trial was a foregone conclusion, and even the Great Defender was unable to stem the tide. Too much was stacked against the wretched man he was trying to save – a forlorn hope. The defendant ranted and raved, his outbursts becoming more and more frequent as the trial proceeded. He called Mrs Crossley a 'raving lunatic' and Detective Inspector Neil 'a scoundrel of the first water' – a ludicrous description indeed, all things considered. 'I don't care twopence what these two say!' he shouted at the judge. 'You cannot sentence me to death. I have done no murder. I have nothing to fear.' He shouted abuse at his counsel, and even had the temerity to interrupt the judge during his summing-up: 'You'll have me hanged the way you're going on! Sentence me and have done with it! It's a disgrace to a Christian country, this is! I'm not a murderer, though I may be a bit peculiar.' That, surely, was the understatement of the year.

Mr Archibald Bodkin's closing speech for the prosecution was brief and to the point; Marshall Hall's was somewhat longer. He had not dared call Smith to the stand in his own defence, and neither had he called any witnesses on his behalf. He had relied on his own power of rhetoric, but that, alas, was powerless to save his client.

On that sweltering July day, as the trial drew to a close, the judge delivered his summing-up. Towards the end of his speech he reminded the participants that beyond the confines of the courtroom the war was being waged and thousands of lives were being lost, both combatants and civilians. 'And yet,' he said, 'while this wholesale destruction of human life is going on, for some days all the apparatus of justice in England has been considering whether just one man should die ...'

At 2.52 p.m. the jury retired to consider their verdict, and after being out for only twenty-two minutes they returned with a unanimous verdict of guilty, and Smith was sentenced to death. He took this quite calmly – a most unexpected attitude after the outbursts he had been capable of – and after sentencing he leaned over the rail of the dock to thank Marshall Hall for his valiant efforts. 'I thank you for everything you have done,' he said. 'I still have great confidence in you. I shall bear up.' His appeal was dismissed, and on 4 August he was moved from Pentonville to Maidstone Prison.

Edith Pegler, who had sat outside the courtroom during the entire trial and wept tears of silent desperation, travelled to Maidstone to be there outside the prison gates when, on a sunny morning which dawned clear on Friday the thirteenth, Smith was taken across the prison yard for his last walk, and was hanged at 8 a.m. in the execution shed; his body was buried in the prison precincts in an unmarked grave.

The following day Caroline Love, née Thornhill, Smith's only legal wife, was notified of his death. She was now a widow, and free to remarry. A Canadian soldier whom she had met in Canada, a sapper with the Royal Engineers, obtained a special licence and married her that same day.

But for Edith Pegler, her life blighted, there was to be no marriage. She had given her heart to an unworthy object, and having discovered that her marriage was false and but a mere sham, she was disillusioned. She returned home to tend her mother, who was in her eighties, until her death. Afterwards she looked after her invalid sister until she, too, passed on. Edith remained in the family home and died a recluse.